FLY-FISHING HANDBOOK

WRITTEN AND ILLUSTRATED BY
DAVE WHITLOCK

L&B

LYONS & BURFORD, PUBLISHERS

Printed in Montréal, Canada

10 9 8 7 6 5 4 3 2 1

Design by M.R.P. Design

Typesetting and composition by CompuDesign

Library of Congress Cataloging-in-Publication Data

Whitlock, Dave

    L.L. Bean fly-fishing handbook / written and illustrated by Dave Whitlock.

       p.   cm.

    Includes bibliographical references and index.

    ISBN 1-55821-437-2

    1. Fly fishing—Handbooks, manuals, etc.   I. Title.

    SH456.W45   1996

    799. 1'2—dc20   96-306

                                    CIP

CONTENTS

ACKNOWLEDGMENTS

Welcome to the special world of fly fishing. In recent years, fly fishing has become increasingly popular as more people discover its magical qualities. After over fifty years of fly-fishing experience, most spent teaching either family, friends, business associates, or the general public, I've come to the conclusion that it is a sport that nearly anyone who loves nature and the outdoors can enjoy. And the ten-plus years that I worked with the L.L. Bean Fly-Fishing Schools were certainly among the most significant that I've experienced learning and teaching the sport.

This handbook is a direct result of those experiences. A lot of people helped me develop these teaching methods as well as this handbook and I'd like to take this opportunity to recognize and thank them.

Leon Gorman and Scott Sanford for giving me the opportunity to represent L.L. Bean and to develop the L.L. Bean Fly-Fishing Schools.

Tom Ackerman, Brock Apfel, and Mike Verville for helping me with school coordination and instruction.

John Bryan, Don Davis, Rob Crawford, Pat Jackson, Dwight Lander, John Meadow, Joe Murray, Joe Robinson, and Joan Whitlock for the very special work they each did as instructors and contributors to the schools and the handbook.

Nick Lyons and his outstanding editorial staff for all the editions of this handbook. Their patience and attention to detail have made my instructions and illustrations much easier to study and use.

My wife, Emily Whitlock, for her encouragement, wonderful advice, superb photography, and editing, which helped make this edition so much more effective for the readers and students of fly fishing.

And my heartfelt thanks to the L.L. Bean Fly-Fishing Schools students for teaching me how to instruct fly fishing with maximum effectiveness . . . and for enriching my life with their time, warmth, enthusiasm, and fishing stories!

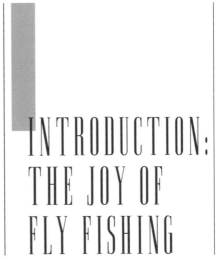

INTRODUCTION: THE JOY OF FLY FISHING

One summer afternoon some years ago, Dave Whitlock and I fly fished up a little feeder creek in Yellowstone Park. It was a warm afternoon and we were in no particular hurry—which is the best way to fish—so we fished together and then alone, and we talked a lot, and we caught a few trout. Dave did most of the catching.

The particular brand of fly fishing we did was unusual and I had not done it before. Big fish had come up into this feeder stream from a larger, famous river whose temperature got quite high in August. The fish, Dave told me, were in the stream for relief from the heat, not food. You had to tempt them with a fly they could not refuse. He suggested a grasshopper, which is a mouthful, and he gave me a new version of his famous Dave's Hopper. Dave is one of America's most innovative fly tyers and—had I been a trout, and as they proved—this fly looked good enough to eat.

Dave showed me how to approach a bend pool, how to stand fifteen feet back from the bank, how to cast so that merely the leader fell on the water. These were special techniques, local refinements. He gently corrected a hitch or two in my casting and helped me perfect a knot—for he is a deft instructor.

About five o'clock, beneath a stand of lodgepole pine, we picked some small wild strawberries, sat on the mossy ground, looked up at a singularly blue sky, talked about the fish we'd seen and caught, compared notes. We were both smiling broadly at the exquisite pleasure of the past few hours. He said he wished everyone had a chance to spend at least one afternoon like this—back in wild country, with a good friend, learning a new technique or two, fly fishing to difficult trout, catching a few. Fly fishing was at the heart of it. Twenty years earlier, I said, before I fly fished, the day would have been impossible. The particular peace and pleasure I felt were intricately connected to the brand of fishing I practiced—the rhythmic cast, with rod and line becoming extensions of my arm; the subtle drop of the fly, which imitated a natural insect; the intimate knowledge of the stream and our quarry that we needed to fish this way. And I was still learning. That was part of fly fishing, too: It became more and more fascinating and (no matter how good you got) there was always something new to learn. The afternoon had been a blend of satisfactions: skills already mastered and new skills that I had learned—none of them difficult to learn, though once I'd thought so.

We used equipment that was balanced and understood. Line, reel, and rod were matched, and could do our bidding. The simple and lovely act of casting a fly—in this case one tied by Dave—was in itself rewarding. We had to stalk the fish, in gorgeous surroundings, and we had to know why they were here and on what they might feed. You could not merely chuck out a bait or lure and chance a fish coming by. We had to "read" the water, know our fish, actively hunt them. We were more closely connected to the subtle web of nature than we could possibly have been through any other pastime I could imagine. We were more involved—physically and mentally—than had we practiced any other fishing method. The wild strawberries we ate—which were soft, bright crimson, astonishingly sweet—were only the most palpable symbol of our connection with the natural world.

Dave and I were ourselves an example of the magic fly fishing weaves. He lives in Arkansas and I in a large eastern city; for him, fly fishing is a way of life, a consummate art to be practiced with cunning and increasing skill; for me it is that, too, but also a respite from the work and tension of cities: As the modern world has become more and more mechanized, crowded, even harsh in its metropolitan pressures, I have grown to love fly fishing the more and to appreciate its gifts, for itself and as a sorely needed tonic. It demands such happy skill of hand and eye, knowledge of the fish's world, imagination; it always challenges and refreshes me. Dave and I were from sharply different worlds—rural and urban—and may even have fly fished for different reasons; but we shared an absolute joy in this special art of angling. Fly fishing had brought us together, taught us a common language, made us friends.

Too many people avoid fly fishing because they think it is too difficult to learn. Some take it up without proper instruction and then drop it. This little handbook is an antidote. It has one simple purpose: to be a clear and eminently practical introduction to the sport. It seeks to take the mystery out of fly fishing and to make it accessible to a vast number of people who might otherwise avoid the sport.

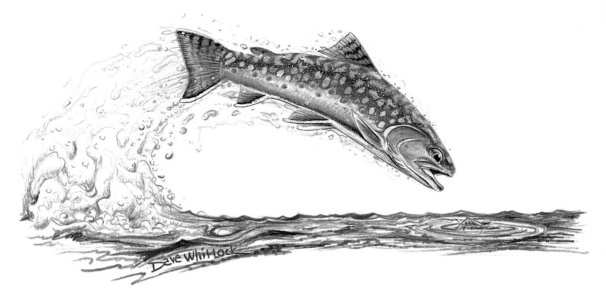

Brook trout leaping down on Dave's Hopper

To my mind, this handbook does the job with unique skill. That's not surprising. For the twenty-five years Dave's been teaching fly fishing, ten have been spent working with the L.L. Bean Fly-Fishing Schools System. It has been a happy and successful venture. With the company's encouragement and support, Dave has developed a variety of new teaching techniques; he has refined his own considerable skills as an instructor; and he has found the simplest and most effective ways to get people started fly fishing. Since his methods worked so well with hundreds of students, L.L. Bean thought they ought to be in print; the result, I think, is like spending a weekend fishing with Dave.

Dave will introduce you to fly tackle, fly casting, fishing tactics, fly tying, and other tools and skills that will make this sport of limitless interest to you, regardless of your age, sex, income, or athletic ability. You will learn that it is not beyond your ability to cast well and with accuracy, and that with a little patience and practice you can tie your own flies—and then catch fish on them—and that this will double your fly-fishing pleasure. Dave will surprise you by showing how many different species can be caught on a fly—not only trout but also bluegill, bass, bluefish, on up to sailfish and even marlin; fly fishing can be practiced not only in rivers but also in ponds, lakes, estuaries, and the ocean. Since Dave is a skilled artist, he has supported his text with a multitude of helpful line drawings and charts. In all, this book can provide the down-to-earth basic instruction you need to get you catching fish on a fly. And this time it's in full color.

Once you've learned the fundamentals, you will want to go on and learn more—for fly fishing can become a finely tuned art. And in a short time you'll know why millions of anglers consider fly fishing the most versatile and challenging—as well as the most enjoyable—way to sportfish. As my afternoon with Dave on that haunting western stream reminded me, it is also a singularly compelling way to enjoy the outdoors.

—Nick Lyons

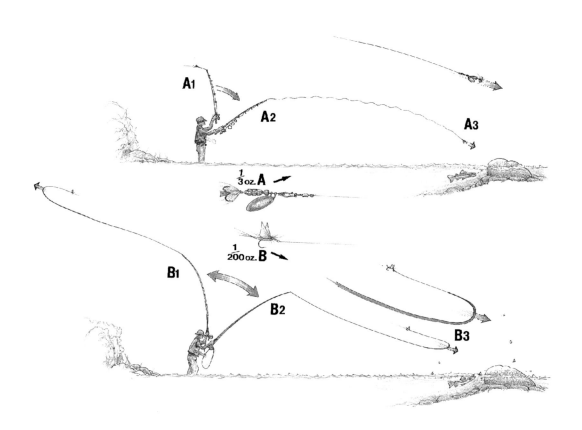

CONVENTIONAL CASTING AND FLY CASTING

In CONVENTIONAL CASTING (called bait casting or plug casting), the rod movement (A1) sends a weighted lure (A3) into motion and the lure then pulls the almost weightless line (A2) after it. In FLY CASTING the rod movement (B1) sends a weighted fly line (B2) into motion and the fly line then pulls the almost weightless fly (B3) after it.

1
UNDERSTANDING FLY TACKLE

Fly fishing is a purely *personal* and manual method of sport-fishing that involves the casting, presentation, and manipulation of an artificial fly to hook, play, and land fish. Fly fishing is unique because the tackle components—rod, reel, line, leader, and fly—are used differently from the ways tackle is used in such other popular angling methods as spin-casting, spinning, and bait-casting. In fly fishing, you use the fly rod to cast a length of handheld, weighted line that propels an almost weightless lure (the fly) to the fishing area. Other methods employ a *propelled* weighted lure to pull an almost weightless line off the reel.

▼

The **fly rod** is designed to control (with mechanical advantage) the uniquely linear-shaped and weighted **fly line.** Fly rods are generally longer and more supple than other fishing rods to allow optimum performance in casting and in leader and fly presentations, as well as in their correct manipulation on water.

The **fly reel's** function is to hold the excess fly line and backing line during casting and fishing. Once a fish is hooked, the reel, acting as a winch, allows line to be extended or retrieved as you play the fish.

The **leader,** a light, nearly invisible extension of the heavy, highly visible fly line, aids in presenting and manipulating the fly.

Flies, which can imitate any type of natural fish food (such as insects, smaller fish, shrimp, leeches, frogs, or even plant parts), are cast and manipulated near the fish with the fly rod and line. The feel, visual pleasure, and control you receive from holding the sensitive rod in one hand and the bare fly line in the other hand while casting, presenting the fly to the target, puppeteering the fly, and then striking and fighting the fish are personal, sensitive experiences that surpass all other methods of fishing.

This seemingly simple manual method actually has nearly limitless possibilities—far more than other methods that use live bait or artificial lures. The most noticeable reason for this is that the fly has no significant weight. This allows the fly fisher to imitate the whole range of fish food sizes, from $1/16$ inch to 10 inches or more.

A fly-fishing outfit has five main tackle components: the fly, the leader, the line, the rod, and the reel. These components work together most efficiently when they are balanced, or matched to one another. Thanks to agreements by fly-tackle manufacturers, most components are uniformly coded with the information you need to assemble well-matched fly tackle.

THE FLY LINE

The **fly line,** with its linear casting weight, is the key component of the fly-tackle system. The fly line appears, to the user of other casting methods, to be unusually thick. This is because weight and taper are built into a fly line to aid in casting and making the line float or sink. Line diameter does not necessarily correspond to line weight or strength, as is the case with the lines used in other angling methods.

Fly-line sizes are standardized; calibrated according to a code adopted by the American Fishing Tackle Manufacturers Association (AFTMA). An AFTMA fly-line size is calculated by weighing the first 30 feet of the line (excluding the tapered tip of the line); lines are measured in grain-weight units from 60 to 850 grains.

Fly lines are available in weights ranging from 1 to 15, with weights 1 through 12 covering most of the fly fisher's needs. The four most popular line weights are 5, 6, 7, and 8. The 6-weight floating line is today's best-selling fly line.

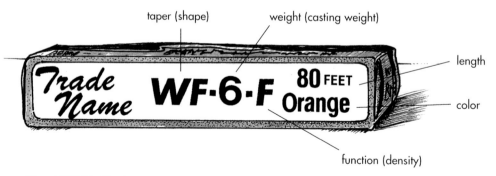

The AFTMA Fly Line Code as it is typically printed on the fly-line box.

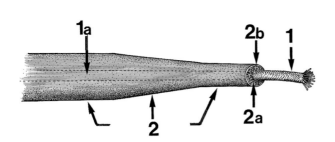

Composition of Modern Fly Line

1. *Braided level core*
1a. *The core gives the fly line most of its strength.*
2. *The coating provides most of the fly-line weight, shape, and size.*
2a. *The compostion of the coating determines fly-line density.*
2b. *The coating finish reduces friction in rod guides, air, and water.*

All modern fly lines are clearly marked and coded on their containers with the AFTMA line weight and other design and use codes. The *design, weight,* and *density* of the fly line determine how the fly is cast and the depth at which the fly is fished.

Most modern fly lines are constructed with a central core of level braided nylon or similar synthetic material. The **core** provides strength, a portion of the line's weight, and the foundation for layers of coating. The **coating** generally consists of one or more layers of a molded PVC plastic or vinyl material and provides the line with a durable shape (or taper), the majority of its weight and flexibility, its density, and its color. The coating also has a very smooth, *low-friction* surface for line movement through the rod's guides, your hands, the air, and water. Some premium fly lines are even impregnated with lubricating agents that gradually seep from the line to make it more friction-free.

Fly-line Densities

There are three main fly-line densities: floating, intermediate, and sinking.

The **floating line** (F), buoyant to ride on top of the water, is usually the first line a beginning fly fisher purchases. It is used primarily when fishing dry flies (floating flies), but it is also often used with wet flies, streamers, or nymphs (sinking flies) in shallow water, generally less than 10 feet.

The **intermediate line** (I) is just slightly heavier than water so that it sinks slowly. This fly line is most useful for fly fishing with wet flies and nymphs at shallow depths for trout, panfish, bass, bonefish, and tarpon. An intermediate line can be dressed with line flotant to make it float. The old silk fly lines were all intermediates and required frequent coating with paraffin to make them float.

Sinking lines can be subdivided into sinking-tip and full-sinking lines.

The **sinking-tip line** (F/S) is just that: The first 5, 10, or 15 feet (the tip) of the line sinks and the remainder of the line (the belly) floats. The sinking-tip line

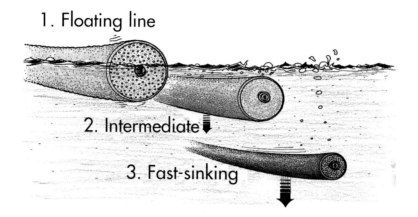

1. Floating line

2. Intermediate

3. Fast-sinking

This cross-sectional diagram shows the water positions of three fly-line densities of the same weight.

is becoming very popular as a second line. It allows you to fish floating/diving flies, wet flies, nymphs, streamers, and bottom-crawling flies with ease, yet it has many of the more desirable casting characteristics of a floating line. It is much easier for beginners to use than a full-sinking line. Sinking-tip lines are excellent for fishing flies at depths of 2 to 10 feet.

Sinking-tip fly lines are available in several tip-density choices, with sinking speeds of slow (I), medium (II), fast (III), or extra-fast (IV and V). Faster-sinking (or higher-density) tips keep the fly deeper during a retrieve or while it is drifting in current.

The **full-sinking line** (S) is used to pull a fly down to a depth of as much as 30 feet. Sinking lines are useful for standard casting and retrieving techniques as well as for trolling. As with sinking-tips, different densities are available to pro-

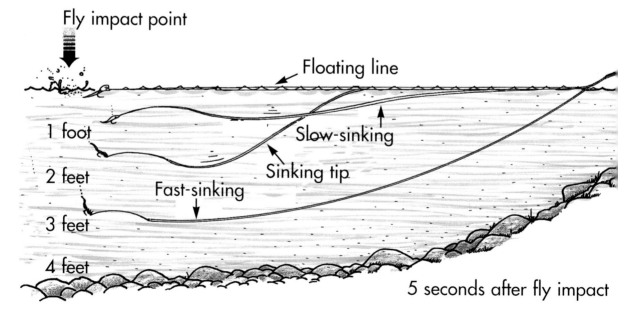

Fly impact point

Floating line

1 foot

Slow-sinking

2 feet

Sinking tip

Fast-sinking

3 feet

4 feet

5 seconds after fly impact

vide a choice of sinking rates from slow to very fast. Most of the density variation is created by impregnating the fly line's coating with lead, tungsten, or other heavy metal particles.

These three main fly-line styles—floating, intermediate, and sinking—of identical AFTMA line weights will have different diameters. The floating line will have the largest diameter and the sinking line the smallest. This is a function of water displacement versus density. Because 30 feet of floating line weighs the same as 30 feet of sinking line, the floating line must be larger in diameter in order to float. The thicker floating line will *feel* lighter than the same weight sinking line, but it is not. It also will not cast quite as far as the sinking line with an equal amount of effort. This happens simply because the floating line's greater surface area creates more drag on the rod's guides and in the air.

The effect of each fly-line density on a fly after five seconds on the water.

Fly-Line Shapes

Most fly lines are made in one of three shapes: level, double taper, or weight forward. Each design has characteristics that you should understand in order to choose the right line for your needs. Although a fly line is more complex in makeup and higher in price than monofilament spinning line or braided bait-casting or trolling line, with proper care it will last considerably longer (usually three or four years) than other fishing lines.

The **level line** (L) has a level braided core and a level molded coating throughout its length. It works well for casting and roll-casting short distances (20 to 40 feet). Because the *tip* of a level line is so heavy and large in diameter compared to the other line shapes, it limits your ability to make delicate or complex presentations. Generally, we do not recommend using a level fly line to learn proper fly-casting and presentation methods.

The **double-taper line** (DT) is tapered for several feet on each end and has a uniform diameter in the midsection. The tapered tip permits more delicate and controlled presentation of the leader and fly than does the uniform tip of the level line. The double taper is well suited for most short- and medium-distance fly casting and roll-casting. Its larger midsection, however, hinders the shooting of line for distance casting (over 60 feet). The double taper has the advantage of a longer life than the other tapered designs, for it can be reversed on the reel when the front tapered end begins to wear out.

The **weight-forward line** (WF) has a tip taper generally identical to the tip of a double-taper line. It has a short, heavy midsection tapering to a long, lighter, level shooting section behind. The weight-forward line casts well at short and intermediate distances, and because of its more advanced design, it will cast farther and more easily than the level or double-taper design. Roll-casting distance, however, is limited to approximately 40 to 50 feet. Beyond that distance, the smaller shooting-line section reduces roll-casting efficiency. Although it cannot be reversed for longer life as the double taper can, the weight-forward line is the most versatile line design.

There are six important modifications of the weight-forward taper: the Long Belly, Rocket Taper, Bass-Bug Taper, Saltwater Taper, Nymph Taper, and Wulff Triangle Taper.

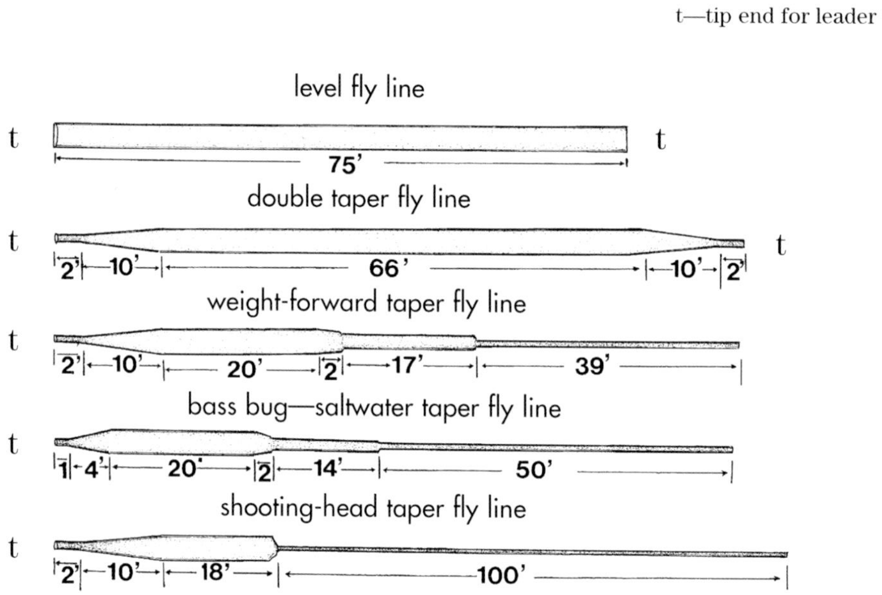

t—tip end for leader

level fly line

double taper fly line

weight-forward taper fly line

bass bug—saltwater taper fly line

shooting-head taper fly line

These are the five most common fly-line shapes.

The **Long Belly** is just that—a longer belly or midsection that enables more line to be carried more easily in the air. Long-belly lines were designed to help make longer casts using modern graphite fly rods.

The **Rocket Taper,** designed by Leon Chandler of the Cortland Line Company, is a weight-forward line with a longer front taper for more delicate presentations, and good roll-casting and shooting performance.

Bass-Bug and **Saltwater Tapers** (floating only) are more or less identical. They have a short, blunt, tip taper with a heavy, short midsection and a long, thinner shooting section. These lines are designed to cast larger, heavier, more wind resistant flies quickly on stiff leaders at short to medium distances (20 to 70 feet) while minimizing false-casts. They are excellent performers in the windy conditions that are so common around bass lakes and salt water.

Nymph Tapers (floating only) are weight-forward lines with a blunt, very buoyant tapered tip specially designed to maximize the casting and mending of sinking nymphs, split shot, and strike indicators. A nymph taper also shoots line easily to minimize false-casting while nymphing.

The **Wulff Triangle Taper** (floating only) is a weight-forward line designed by Lee Wulff. It has a continuous tapering belly or midsection designed to load the rod well and carry the energy to the loop very efficiently. Because this concept is so different from that of standard level-belly weight forwards, triangle-taper lines have a very distinctive feel. These lines also have an ease of roll-casting.

The **shooting-head line** (SH) is a special-purpose modification of the tapered or level line. To create a shooting-head line, the first 30 feet (the *head*) of a level or tapered line is spliced to 100 feet of 20- to 30-pound-test monofilament or to a special, very small diameter level fly line (the *shooting* line). The shooting head, with its nearly frictionless shooting line, is designed for casting

Long Belly

Rocket Taper

Wulff Triangle Taper

Nymph Taper

Other weight-forward designs (specialized).

long distances (70 to 120 feet). The shooting head is relatively difficult to use, however, and is not a good choice for beginners.

Fly-Line Colors

The visibility of the fly line to the angler affects overall fly-fishing performance and success. White, pastel, or fluorescent lines are easier for the fly fisher to see than dark or neutral color, such as brown, green, or gray. This allows greater control over casting and fishing the fly. But lighter colors are more visible to the fish, which increases the chance of scaring them. In bright light, a fly line in the air actually looks larger than it is, and when a fly line is on or beneath the water, the fish may see it as an unnatural object and become frightened. Dark or neutral colors are less visible above and on the water, so there are some real choices to make.

We recommend that the beginning fly fisher choose a highly visible line to enhance the learning of basics in casting, presentation, and fishing techniques.

Fly-line colors:
1. *Hi Viz for maximum visibility, accuracy, and line control.*
2. *Pastels for good visibility, accuracy, and line control, yet less offensive to fish than Hi Viz.*
3. *Dark colors for low visibility and maximum casting and fishing stealth.*

Fly-Line Weights

The size, or weight, of the fly line you choose should be based on the flies you are going to use (hook size, weight, and wind resistance). Generally speaking, the smaller line sizes (1, 2, 3, 4, and 5 weights) are best suited to flies tied on size 8 to 28 hooks. The medium line sizes (6, 7, and 8) are best for size 1/0 to 12 flies. The large line sizes (9, 10, 11, and 12) are best for size 5/0 to 4 flies. Keep in mind that very wind resistant or heavily weighted flies will require a larger line size than these general parameters. Windy conditions may also make it necessary to use a line one or two weights heavier to cast the same fly correctly. The line size choice is determined by the line's ability to control the fly. If the fly controls the line, you will have casting problems.

For the best line to begin your fly fishing—say for the first one to three years—we recommend a floating, *weight-forward, 6 or 7 weight,* if you plan to seek good instruction from a professional or a fly-fishing school. If this type of assistance is not available to you, we recommend a *floating double taper,* which is initially easier to use. Six- or 7-weight fly lines and matched fly tackle are the most practical for all-around fly fishing in fresh water.

THE LEADER

The leader provides a low-visibility link between the heavy fly-line tip and the fly. Of almost equal importance, the leader should also assist the fly line's front taper in casting and presenting the fly and letting the fly float, swim, or sink in the most natural manner. To do this, the leader must continue the line tip's taper down its length to its tip. The tapered leader has three parts—the butt, midsection, and tip.

The **butt** section is the largest in diameter, and it resembles the fly-line tip in flexibility and density—continuing the taper of the fly line.

The **midsection** continues the leader's length for deception; it also provides the most drastic taper area.

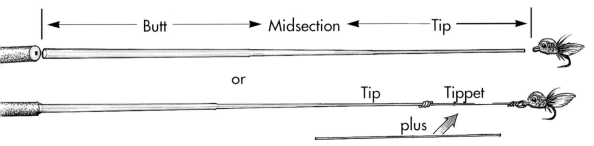

Top: Basic tapered leader parts
Bottom: Optional tippet section attached

The **tip** joins the tapering midsection with a smaller-diameter length of level monofilament. The tip is usually 12 to 24 inches long; this provides the maximum fish-deceiving length while helping to allow a natural movement to the fly in the water. To extend or prolong the tapered leader's life or uses, additional monofilament may be tied to the leader's tip. This addition is called the **tippet.** Though its purpose is simple, it often confuses the new fly fisher.

Understanding The Tippet

The tippet can be used simply to lengthen the leader, or it can be used to add a smaller-diameter section of monofilament to improve fish deception or to allow the use of a smaller fly. A tippet may also be added to repair or replace part of the tip.

Wind knots often occur in the tip or tippet during the course of a day's fishing, as does abrasion damage or breakage. These conditions are corrected by cutting out the problem section and replacing it with a new one. The tippet is usually 18 to 24 inches long. Tippet material is sold in convenient, pocket-sized spools, individually or in sets, with about 10 to 25 yards of material on each spool. The spools are usually well marked to indicate monofilament diameter and breaking strength. It's a good idea to use tippet material of the same make

Tippet Spool detail. Label indicates tippet size, diamet pound test strength, and amount of tippet on spool.

LEADER TIPPET AND FLY SIZE			
(For optimum casting, presentation, and fishing performance)			
Leader Tip or Tippet	**X Code**	**Pound Test**	**Fly-Hook Sizes**
(Diameter in thousandths of an inch)			
.003	8X	1.2	24,26,28,32
.004	7X	2	20,22,24,26
.005	6X	3	16,18,20,22
.006	5X	4	14,16,18
.007	4X	6	12,14,16
.008	3X	8	10,12,14
.009	2X	10	6,8,10
.010	1X	12	2,4,6
.011	0X	14	1/0,2,4
.012	X1	15	2/0,1/0,2
.013	X2	16	3/0,2/0,1/0,2
.014	X3	18	5/0,4/0,3/0,2/0
.015	X4	20	6/0,5/0,4/0,3/0

Based on monofilament nylon, Aeon, and L.L. Bean product

Note: This chart is a simple guideline. Fly-hook wire sizes, hook-shank lengths, extra weighting, and material designs, as well as variations in leader-material stiffness, all affect performance. In situations where water is very clear and calm and fish are very selective, longer, smaller-diameter leaders and tippets are more effective because they are less visible and allow the fly to look and act more natural.

Bite tippet

Leader with bite tippet and fly attached

as the leader. Different tippet brands may be softer or harder than your leader; a mismatch will weaken knots.

A **shock,** or **bite,** tippet is a short section (3 to 12 inches long) of very heavy monofilament (30- to 100-pound test) or metal wire that is added at the fly to prevent fish with sharp teeth or body parts from cutting off the fly. A bite tippet is used for such species as bluefish, tarpon, shark, barracuda, muskellunge, and pike.

Types of Leaders

The **knotted compound-tapered** leader is made by tying together sections of nylon monofilament that differ in diameter to create a desired taper and length. The ability to tie your own tapered leaders can save you money and allow you to experiment with tapers. A drawback, however, is that knots can catch on rod guides or plant life, which can cause fish loss, casting tangles, and leader breakage.

The **braided leader** has a butt and midsection of braided strands of monofilament and a knotted or glued tip section of level nylon monofilament. The **twisted leader** is similar except the strands are twisted rather than braided.

Although braided and twisted leaders are designed to be more flexible and cast better, we have not found this to be the case in most situations.

The **knotless tapered** leader, a continuous length of extruded tapering monofilament, is the most popular and least troublesome design in our experiences

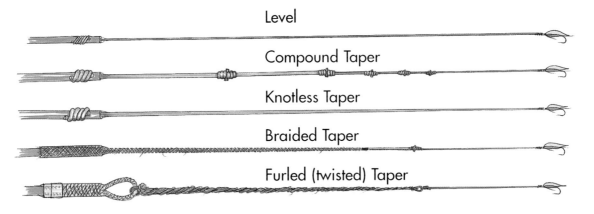

Level

Compound Taper

Knotless Taper

Braided Taper

Furled (twisted) Taper

Five common leader designs

FLY LINE AND LEADER CHART

Type of Fly Line	Leader Length (Feet)	Where to Use
Floating (L, DT, WF)	6 to 7 1/2	Narrow, weedy, brushy creeks (15 to 20 feet wide and small ponds
Floating (L, DT, WF)	7 1/2 to 9	Most creeks, streams, ponds, and lakes
Floating (L, DT, WF)	9, 12, 16	Very clear, calm, shallow, slow-moving spring creeks, ponds, and lakes
Floating Bass and Salt Water (WF)	7 1/2 to 9	Most bass, pike, and panfish streams, ponds, lakes, and saltwater areas
Sinking Tip (WF)	4 to 6	Most waters listed above from 3 to 10 feet deep
Full Sinking (WF, SH)	2 to 6	Most waters listed above 4 to 30 feet deep

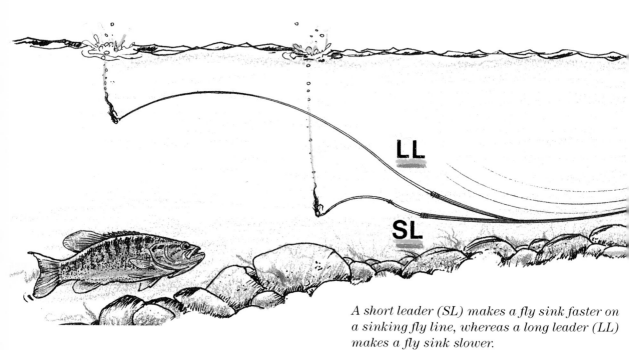

A short leader (SL) makes a fly sink faster on a sinking fly line, whereas a long leader (LL) makes a fly sink slower.

at the L.L. Bean Fly-Fishing Schools and for actual fly fishing. Knotless tapered leaders provide greater freedom from casting tangles, snags, and knot or glue failures.

Level leaders function reasonably well if precise presentation is not necessary, especially short ones (2 to 6 feet) used on sinking-tip or full-sinking fly lines.

Tapered leaders are made in 4-, 6-, $7^{1}/_{2}$-, 9-, 10-, 12-, and 16-foot lengths. The longer leaders, $7^{1}/_{2}$ through 16 feet, are generally used with floating lines. The $7^{1}/_{2}$-foot leader is good for very narrow streams, waters with a rough surface, or murky waters. The 9-foot length is best for general conditions. The 12- and 16-foot lengths are best for very clear waters with calm surfaces.

For sinking-tip and full-sinking fly lines, 2-, 4-, and 6-foot lengths are most useful. Because nylon monofilament is only slightly more dense than water and thus resists sinking, the shorter the leader, the more effective the sinking portion of the line will be in bringing the fly to the desired depth.

Most knotless tapered leaders are sold today as All-Purpose leaders or specific-purpose leaders, such as Nymph, Bass, Saltwater, or Sinking Line. The All-Purpose leader is generally recommended for beginning fly fishers; as your skills and interest increase, the specific-purpose leaders become preferable.

Fluorocarbon Leaders and Tippets

Recently a new alternative to nylon monofilament has been introduced that promises some truly significant improvements for leaders and tippets. The technical name is polyvinylidene fluoride, or more simply, fluorocarbon. Compared to the best nylon it is less visible, denser (sinks faster), more abrasion-resistant, unaffected by ultraviolet radiation, and has better knot strength when wet.

However, compared to nylon, at this point in time it is more expensive, harder to tie knots with, not as strong, and only available in level filaments. Tapered leaders must be hand-tied. Fluorocarbon is probably most practical as an alternative material when its specific properties are needed over those of nylon.

BACKING

Backing is a length of braided line that is attached and wound on to the reel spool and then attached to the end of the fly line.

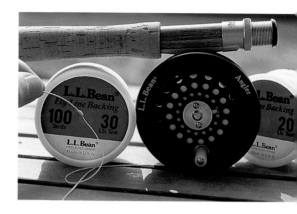

The purpose of backing is to provide extra line in case a fish is strong enough to pull off more than the fly line (a fly line is usually 80 to 120 feet long). Backing also serves to fill the reel spool's excess capacity. This setup allows the reel to retrieve the fly line more efficiently and also allows the fly line to be stored on the reel

Fly-line backing

in relatively large coils. These large coils make straightening the fly line easier, and a straight, coilless fly line casts and fishes better.

The amount of backing used is dictated by the reel-spool capacity, the fly-line size, and how far a fish might run when hooked. We recommend that any fly reel have at least 50 yards of backing on it. Twenty-pound test is best for smaller line weights (1 to 6), and 30-pound test for line sizes 7 to 12.

The ideal line for backing is braided, low-stretch Dacron or Kevlar (12-, 20-, or 30-pound test) attached to the reel spool and then to the end of the fly line. Braided nylon fishing line will also work. *Never* use nylon monofilament for backing as it is prone to tangles and can damage the reel spool.

THE FLY ROD

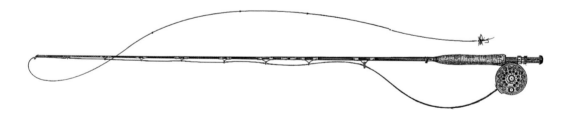

The traditional symbol of the sport, the long, slender, and graceful fly rod is second only to the fly line in importance. The responsive fly rod gives you the control and feel that make casting, fishing, and catching fish on flies so much fun.

The fly rod transfers energy and control from the fly fisher to the line, leader, and fly. Rod length, taper, and action are specifically designed for this purpose. Bait-casting or spinning rods will not perform well for fly fishing.

The fly rod must be matched with the correct fly-line weight for optimum performance in fly casting and presentation. Most fly rods manufactured in the past twenty-five years have the correct line-matching information printed on them just forward of the handle and hookkeeper. Usually, the line-weight range is given along with the rod's length and approximate weight.

Specifications listed on fly rod include rod length and recommended line weight.

The accompanying illustration shows the typical rod specification markings: Model Code Number 907, 9-foot, $3\frac{1}{8}$ ounces, 7-weight line. (Note that the Model Code Number 907 indicates a 9-foot rod and a 7-weight line.) Some manufacturers recommend two line weights. The lighter size usually is for more delicate presentations or for sinking or sinking-tip lines. The heavier is better for floating lines, windy conditions, and casting larger flies.

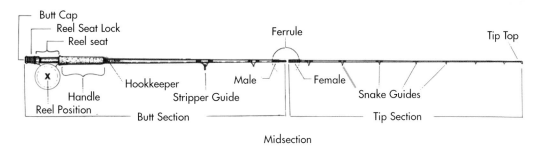

There are seven parts to a fly rod:

The **butt** section is the part of the rod from the handle to one-third of the rod's length. The stiffest part of the rod, the butt mainly adds length and strength to the rod and creates leverage.

The **midsection** is the middle third of the rod's length. This section generally contains the flexing or casting power of the rod.

The **tip** is the top third of the rod's length and is the most flexible part. The tip is principally for shock absorption when striking and landing fish.

The **handle** includes the butt cap, the reel-lock seat for attaching the fly reel in place, the cork grip (also called the handle or rod-hand grip), and the handle check cap. Some heavier rods also have a **fighting** or **extension butt** immediately behind the reel seat.

There are three basic designs of reel seats: *down-locking, up-locking,* and *slide band.* The up-locking reel seat is generally the most dependable choice.

The **hookkeeper** is a wire ring or other simple device that holds the fly's hook safely in place when the outfit is rigged but the angler is not fishing.

The **guides** hold and control the line on the rod during casting. The guides include the *stripper* (or stripping) guide, which is the first guide up the rod from the rod handle and which should be made of a low-friction, hard material. The stripper guide's large inside diameter reduces friction, tangles, and surface wear between line and guide. The *snake* guides hold the fly line close to the rod during casting. Snake guides are light and nearly friction-free to allow easy casting and retrieving of line. The *tip-top* guide holds the fly line at the end of the rod, and, like the other guides, it is designed to be practically friction-free and also to prevent tangling of the line on the end of the rod.

Fly-rod reel seat types: (left to right) slide band, down-locking, up-locking, up-locking with small extension or fighting butt.

Hookkeeper

The **ferrule** is a connection between rod sections. This allows the long fly rod to be easily disassembled for storage. Most fly rods are two- or three-piece, but some break down into as many as six sections for storage or packing convenience. Most ferrules on modern graphite fly rods are made of graphite composites that are lighter and flex more than the older metal ferrule designs.

Most modern fly rods are made of from one of three materials. Each material has different performance characteristics and different production costs.

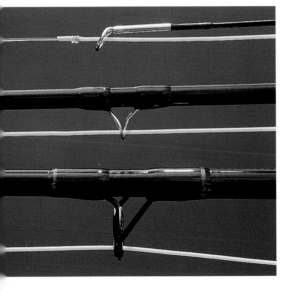

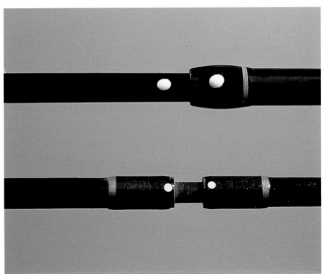

*y-rod guides: (top to bottom) tip
p, snake guide, stripper guide.*

*Fly-rod ferrules: sleeve ferrule
(top), spigot ferrule (bottom).*

The right fly rod for you depends on the type of fishing you will be doing, your level of skill in fly fishing, and what you can afford. The three rod materials are bamboo, fiberglass, and graphite. Combinations of graphite, glass, boron, and/or Kevlar are sometimes used to manufacture composite rods.

Today's **bamboo** or **split-cane rods** are combinations of traditional craftsmanship and modern technology. Those built from high-quality Tonkin cane are lovely to look at and can be very enjoyable to fish with. They are expensive, however, and require considerable care. Those impregnated with special resins tend to require less care, seldom warp, and are more durable. Practically speaking, however, the bamboo fly rod is only for those who are willing to trade light weight and performance of graphite rods for beauty, feel, craftsmanship, and aesthetics. Lighter line-weight bamboo fly rods (2 to 5 weights) are the most practical for fly fishing today.

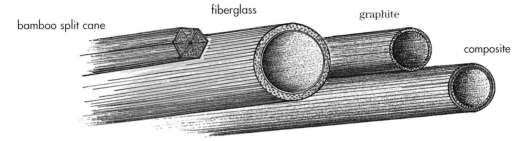

bamboo split cane

fiberglass

graphite

composite

FLY ROD BLANK MATERIALS

All four blank diameters are in the perspective of one fly-line weight. Colors are usually natural; some rods are painted to give a more interesting or attractive fishy finish.

Fiberglass rods replaced bamboo in popularity, durability, and affordability after World War II. Today they are becoming more rare than bamboo rods due to the greater popularity of graphite fly rods.

Graphite (carbon fiber) rods completely dominate the fly-rod market. They are lighter, more sensitive, more powerful, and more forgiving than either bamboo or glass rods. Each year better and more reasonably priced carbon fibers are being manufactured, and graphite fly rods are constantly being improved. Well-made, inexpensive models make it possible for anyone to own an excellent-casting fly rod. I highly recommend graphite for your first fly rod.

Rod Action

The "feel" of a fly rod when it is flexed, cast, mended with, or used to hook and battle a fish is generally described as the rod's *action* or *performance*. This feel is of considerable interest to fly fishers at all levels. The main categories of action are fast, medium, and slow.

> **Fast-action** rods feel stiff when flexed. When the fly line is cast, the rod unflexes or straightens rapidly.

> **Medium-action** rods are more limber when flexed than fast-action, unflex a little slower, and seem smoother. A medium-action rod bends more than a fast-action under the same line weight.

> **Slow-action** rods are very limber and feel rather willowy as they flex and unflex. A slow-action rod bends much more than a fast- or medium-action, especially in the mid- and butt sections.

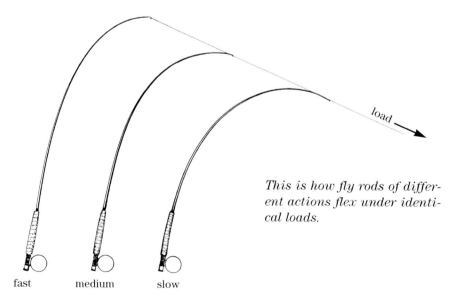

This is how fly rods of different actions flex under identical loads.

load

fast   medium   slow

Regardless of their action, all fly rods should flex progressively from tip to butt under varying loads. This flex produces excellent performance at casting distances of 20 to 80 feet and casts a wide range of fly sizes and weights. When you are fishing the fly, the tip is used to move and animate the fly. When you are setting the hook on a fish, the tip is the principal energy absorber. The midsection and the butt are the energy transmitters. Once the fish is hooked, the rod becomes a lifting and pulling tool. It also transmits the fish's movements to your hand and absorbs the shock of the fish's more violent movements.

The Most Versatile Fly Rod For Beginners

A medium-action, progressively loading fly rod is the best rod with which to learn the sport. Medium action is the most adaptable to a person's individual timing and reflexes. The beginner's rod should be 8 to 8½ feet long, designed to cast a 6- or 7-weight line. This combination is light, sensitive, and provides ample power to cast from 20 to 60 feet. With it you can fish most flies designed for trout, panfish, and small- to medium-sized bass.

After you begin to master the basic fly-casting strokes, qualified instructors will be able to advise you on which action best suits your own reflexes and coordination level. Generally, the quicker your own reaction time, the faster the rod action that will suit you. A person who tends to be relaxed and to have a smooth, slow reaction is better suited to a medium- or slow-action rod; someone with very quick reflexes will probably be more successful with a fast-action rod. Once you are properly matched with a rod, your skill as a caster should progress rapidly. As your casting skill improves, you will be able to cast well with a wider range of fly-rod actions, lengths, line weights, and fly sizes.

THE FLY REEL

The primary function of a fly reel is to contain the backing, the fly line, and the leader. Other functions are to retrieve line and aid in fighting fish. While you are fighting a fish, the reel provides a variable degree of resistance (called drag) that helps tire a strong-swimming fish as it pulls line off the reel. A fly reel, unlike spinning or casting reels, performs no casting function.

The reel is positioned and locked onto the fly rod directly behind and under the rod-hand grip. In this position it counterbalances the rod's weight during casting and fishing and so helps prevent hand and arm fatigue. It also eliminates most fly-line tangles. There are three basic types of fly reels: the single-action, the multiplier, and the automatic.

Types of Reels

The **single-action** reel is a simple direct-drive winch with a one-to-one ratio. One complete revolution of the reel's handle causes the reel spool to make one complete revolution.

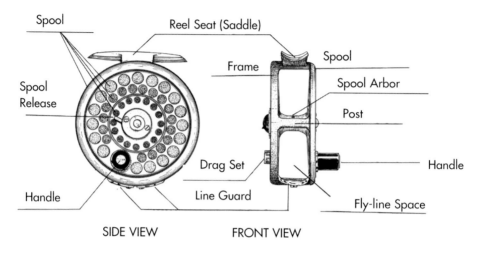

The parts of a typical single-action fly reel.

A well-designed single-action fly reel should be lightweight and corrosion resistant. It should have an adjustable drag to prevent line from free-spooling when it is pulled out by the angler or a fish. Another useful component is an exposed, flanged spool for palming or finger-dragging to increase pressure on a running fish. An audible-click drag is useful to let you hear how fast a fish is taking out line.

A single-action reel should also have interchangeable spools. A properly sized spool will hold the fly line that matches the rod you intend to use, plus 50 to 100 yards of backing. A spool with perforated sides is lighter than one with solid sides, and allows wet line to dry when stored on the spool.

The **multiplier** reel is similar in design to a single-action reel, except that it has a complex, geared winch with a one-to-greater-than-one handle-to-spool ratio. One turn of the handle causes the spool to revolve one and a half to three times. Such a fly reel is most useful when fast or long line retrieves are routinely necessary.

The **automatic** reel is designed to rewind line automatically. If you have ever used a roller type of pull-down window shade, you know the principle. As you pull fly line off the reel, the action puts tension on a built-in coil spring. Then you can quickly and mechanically wind the line back onto the spool by lifting a spool-spring tension lever.

Fly reels: (left to right) single action, multiplier, and automatic.

The automatic fly reel has very limited capacity for line and backing and offers no quick-change, extra-spool options. Because of its spring-loading design, it has a very coarse and nonadjustable drag system. Only a limited amount of fly line can be pulled directly off the reel without releasing the spring tension. This limitation is troublesome if you need to pull additional line or backing off the reel. The automatic is quite heavy and mechanically unreliable in many fly-fishing situations. It is best suited for fly fishing where short casting is used, fast retrieves are needed, and the fish does not take line off the reel. However, people who have the use of only one hand or a disabled hand can fly fish successfully with the automatic fly reel.

The **single-action reel** is the most popular and practical choice for most fly fishing. We recommend this type of reel in a size that will hold a 6- or 7-weight fly line and the appropriate amount of backing.

FLIES

The **fly** is an artificial lure designed either to imitate natural fish foods or to otherwise stimulate a fish into striking. The term *fly* stems from fly fishing's origins in Europe where live insects impaled on hooks were used to catch trout, grayling,

BEGINNER'S OUTFIT
The outfit I recommend for most people over fourteen years old is a 6- or 7-weight, 8$\frac{1}{2}$-foot graphite two-piece fly rod with a medium-fast action; single-action fly reel with 50 to 100 yards of 20-pound-test Dacron backing; and a floating weight-for-ward 6- or 7-weight fly line with a 7$\frac{1}{2}$- or 9-foot knotless tapered leader. This is the best all-around outfit for all things—flies, fish, your strength, and conditions. For a younger or smaller person, an 8-foot, 5- or 6-weight rod and line is best.

and other species. Later, artificial imitations of live insects were conceived. Today, the term *fly* doesn't necessarily mean an imitation of an insect, but rather is a term that covers a wide variety of artificial fishing lures.

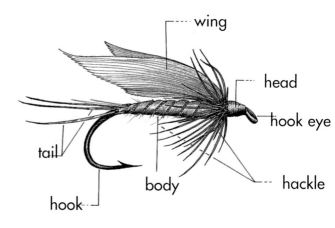

Artificial fly parts

The fly seldom weighs more that $\frac{1}{32}$ ounce and usually weighs less than $\frac{1}{64}$ ounce. Fly lengths are from $\frac{1}{16}$ inch to 10 inches. Flies are handmade, usually on a single, light hook using lightweight, natural and synthetic materials such as feathers, furs, threads, flosses, latex, plastics, wood, foam rubber, and waterproof cements.

There are five important aspects in a good artificial fly: size, action, shape, color, and odor. Each of these is sensed and investigated by the fish before it is lured into trying to eat the fraud.

Size is extremely important, especially so when the food a fly imitates is less than an inch long. **Action** is important, too, for a fly must seem alive or otherwise in a natural state. **Shape** adds an impressionistic or realistic imitation of the food form. **Color** enhances the imitation by increasing visual recognition and attracting the fish. Though flies are not usually "scented" with fish food odors, it is important that the fly have a neutral or natural **odor** not disliked by fish.

Types of Flies

The two general types of fly designs are floating (dry) flies and sinking (wet) flies.

The **floating,** or **dry,** fly rides on or in the water's surface. Floating flies come in a wide range of sizes, color patterns, and shapes, and may imitate aquatic or terrestrial insects, small animals, reptiles, amphibians, or even plant seeds.

The floating fly's effectiveness is determined by its shape, the material from which it is made, and how it is manipulated by the angler on the water's surface. The flies listed below can be fished many ways, from sitting motionless on the surface to fluttering, wiggling, popping, diving, or skipping across the surface. These lifelike actions imitate natural floating foods and so attract the fish.

Floating flies are usually effective during warmer weather when both terrestrial (land-based) and aquatic (water-based) foods are more active and abundant. Adult aquatic insects (such as mayflies, caddisflies, and midges) and

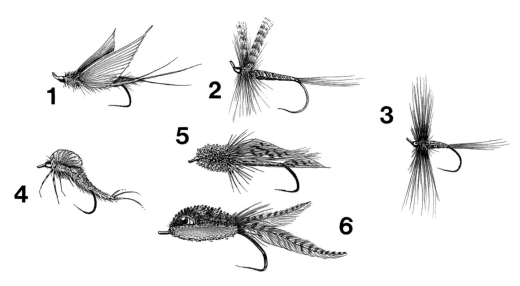

Floating fly examples

1. No-Hackle Dry Fly
2. Hackled Dry Fly
3. Skater Dry Fly
4. Floating-Emergent Nymph
5. Muddler Minnow
6. Deer Hair Frog

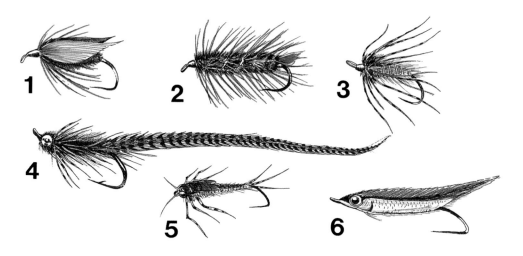

Sinking fly examples

1. Wet Fly
2. Woolly Worm
3. Soft-Hackle Fly
4. Eelworm
5. Nymph
6. Matuka-Mylar Streamer

terrestrial insects (such as ants, grasshoppers, and beetles) are far more active during warmer weather. At times, minnows and nymphs (immature aquatic insects) also gather at the water's surface to feed, to flee underwater predators, or to hatch (nymphs). During times of such surface activity, floating flies that imitate what are normally subsurface foods can be effective. Floating-fly designs include:

1. Hackled dry flies	7. Spiders
2. No-hackle dry flies	8. Skaters
3. Wakers	9. Divers
4. Bass poppers	10. Sponge bugs
5. Hair bugs	11. Floating nymphs
6. Muddlers	12. Terrestrial insects

Sinking, or **wet,** flies are designed to imitate a wide range of submerged terrestrial or aquatic organisms. Sinking flies may also be designed to stimulate a reflex response that makes fish strike.

Sinking-fly materials are either water absorbent or heavier than water, so the fly sinks. The fly's shape and density and the fishing method used determine how deep it is fished. Sinking-fly designs include:

1. Traditional wet flies	8. Bucktails
2. Soft-hackle flies	9. Woolly Worms
3. Nymphs	10. Eelworm streamers
4. Streamers	11. Leeches
5. Egg flies	12. Emergers
6. Attractors	13. Woolly Buggers
7. Worms	14. Crayfish

Sinking flies are more effective than floating flies overall because most of the time fish feed under the water's surface. That's because underwater food is generally more abundant and easier for the fish to detect. Besides, a fish feeding under the surface exposes itself to fewer predators than one feeding on the surface.

2
ASSEMBLING FLY TACKLE

It is easy to assemble fly tackle *properly,* but at first the several components of the tackle system—the rod, reel, backing, fly line, leader, tippet, and fly—might seem confusing. With practice, it will all become second nature.

▼

The accompanying diagrams should give you a clear picture of how to set up the complete tackle system used in most fly fishing. You might find it valuable also to seek out the help of someone who already fly fishes.

The instructions are divided into two parts: first the initial reel and line-components assembly, using the fly-rod butt section, and then the complete assembly for actual fishing.

FLY-LINE SYSTEM COMPONENT ASSEMBLY

The first thing to do is learn the knots and connections of the fly-line system. Strong, small, smooth, easy-to-make junctions are absolutely necessary for high performance. The connections that I recommend and use myself are neat, strong, and easy to do yourself. I think they are among the best yet developed.

Study the diagram. Notice that there are six parts to the fly-line system: the fly reel, braided backing, fly line, leader, tippet, and fly. To join these parts efficiently, there are five connections. For four of these, the same knot is used—the Duncan loop (also called the uni-knot). For the other connection, the tippet to leader, use the double surgeon's knot.

The connections we will be making are: 1. Backing to reel; 2. Backing to fly line; 3. Leader to fly line; 4. Tippet to leader tip; 5. Tippet end to fly.

To set up your system, select a well-lighted tabletop surface and a comfortable

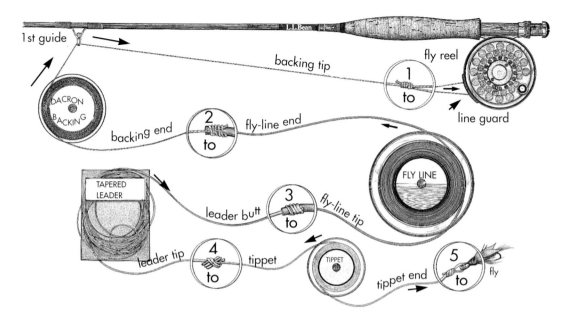

The components and the five connections of the fly-line system.

chair. Have on hand a small pair of needle-nose pliers with smooth jaws, scissors, fingernail clippers, several size 8 to 10 darning needles, a needle vise or an L.L. Bean Knot Tool Kit, and an emery stone. Have ready your fly rod's handle section, fly reel, a spool of backing, fly line, leader, tippet material, and a large fly or hook.

Remove the fly-rod butt section from its protective tube and cloth case. Check your reel to make sure that its drag system is set to operate correctly when used with the hand with which you intend to hold its handle. Most new fly reels are convertible to right- or left-hand wind. Most come from the manufacturer set up to operate with right-hand wind. If you wish to use the other hand, refer to the reel's instructions or ask a knowledgeable friend or salesperson to help you convert the reel. I *strongly* recommend that you use the hand you do *not* cast the rod with to control the fly reel—that is, if you cast right-handed, retrieve with your left hand. With this arrangement, you need not switch hands after casting to begin fighting a fish or retrieving line.

Backing to Reel

Place the fly reel on the fly-rod handle with the reel handle on the side that you intend to use for retrieve and the reel's *line guard* facing forward. Tighten the reel seat so that the reel does not rock from side to side or move forward or backward. Use finger pressure only—avoid using a wrench or pliers to tighten the reel-seat lock rings. When the reel is mounted on the rod, you can easily reel on backing, line, and leader because the rod butt provides a convenient handle.

The next step is to put the backing on the reel. Remove 5 or 6 feet of backing from the spool and place its tag end down through the stripper guide toward the handle, then through the reel's line guard, and finally twice around the spool spindle. (This is simpler and faster to do if you remove the reel spool from the reel's frame. Be sure to pass the line through the line guard before attaching it to the spool.)

Make sure that the backing end passes in and out at the same place and not between one or two of the reel's frame posts; otherwise, you'll find it impossible to tie the line to the spool. Pull at least 12 inches of backing through the reel; this will be enough to tie the Duncan loop. (See diagram *Backing to Reel.*) *Be sure you snug the knot tightly down on the spool's spindle; it must not slip on it.*

Knot #1: Backing to Fly Reel with Duncan Loop

1. Pass the backing line through the line guard of the reel and then twice around the reel spool and back out to the line guard—leaving 8 to 12 inches of tag end for the knot.

2. Form a large loop with the tag end toward and then away from the reel.

3. The tag excess should now be about 6 to 8 inches long.

4. With the tag end, make four wraps away from the reel, through the loop and standing line, as shown here.

5. Pull on the **tag** to tighten the knot over the line.

6. Pull hard on the line to slide and tighten the line against the spool spindle. Clip off the excess tag end. Make sure that the knot loop is absolutely tight against the spindle.

You are now ready to wind the backing onto the reel spool. Place a pencil, pen, or wooden dowel through the center hole of the backing spool. If help is available, have someone hold the backing spool by the pencil; if alone, place the pencil between your knees for control and tension. *Always wind the reel's handle forward*—clockwise with your right hand, counterclockwise with your left. Use just enough tension between backing spool and reel spool to ensure that the backing is firmly wrapped on the fly-reel spool.

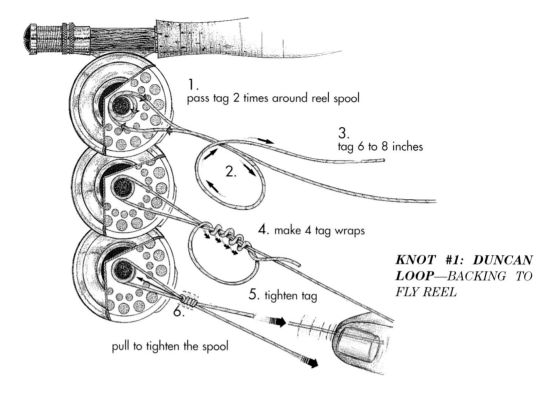

1. pass tag 2 times around reel spool

2.

3. tag 6 to 8 inches

4. make 4 tag wraps

5. tighten tag

6.

pull to tighten the spool

KNOT #1: DUNCAN LOOP—BACKING TO FLY REEL

As you wind on backing, try to position the consecutive winds on the spool evenly, going from one side to the other and back. Use your rod hand's index finger to control tension and position the backing on the spool.

You should fill the spool with backing to a level that leaves enough space to hold the fly line plus a fingertip's clearance between the reel post and fly line. This may be hard to judge. If you're in doubt, ask an experienced fly fisher or your tackle dealer how much backing your particular reel needs with the fly line you have. Remember, a floating line takes up more space than the same weight and length of sinking line.

Backing to Fly line

After placing the proper amount of backing on the reel, you are ready to attach the fly line to the backing. If the fly line is wound on a plastic storage spool, find the end and pull off about 24 inches of fly line. If the fly line is only coiled loosely around the plastic spool, carefully remove any twist-ties, then find the end and pull out the fly-line length. Most manufacturers include in the container directions for unspooling their fly line. With a weight-forward line, you must tie the backing to the back or shooting portion of the fly line; most manufacturers mark this with a small printed tab. For level or double-taper fly lines, it does not matter which end you use first. However, try to locate the top or upper end for easiest unwinding.

To attach the backing to the fly-line end, follow the *Backing to Fly Line* diagram, which is simply a modification of the *Backing to Reel* knot.

Knot #2: Backing to Fly Line with Duncan Loop

1. Lay 10 inches of backing alongside the end of the fly line.

2. Loop the tag end back toward the fly-line end to form a 2-inch loop.

3. The tag end of the backing should be 5 or 6 inches long.

4. With the tag end of the backing, make five wraps over the fly line and through the loop back from the fly-line end.

5. Grasp the fly line and wraps, then carefully pull on both sides of the backing to close the slack in the loop. Take care not to allow the knot to slip off the end of the fly line.

6. Pull on the tag end to tighten the knot wraps and loop firmly against the end of the fly line. Try to keep the knot wraps close together but not overlapping.

7. Pull the backing tight and trim the excess fly line and backing so that you have a neat, trouble-free knot. Coat the knot and fly-line end with a flexible waterproof cement to make the connection smoother and stronger.

With the backing attached to the fly line, carefully wind it onto the reel spool, firmly but not tightly. Leave about 4 feet of the fly line loose off the reel for the leader-to-fly-line connection. Should your reel spool be too full of back-

KNOT #2: DUNCAN LOOP—BACKING TO FLY LINE

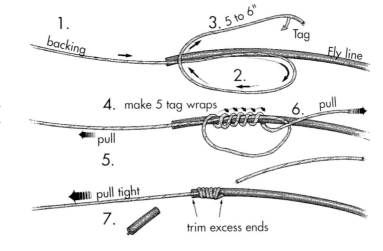

ing to accept the entire fly line with room for your little finger between the fly line and the reel's frame posts, you must do one of two things: Remove the fly line, cut the backing-to-fly-line knot, and remove some part of the backing so that the fly line fits the spool; or, if you are putting on a level or weight-forward line, you can cut off as much as 10 to 12 feet from the level running line without affecting casting or fishing performance. The advantage of the latter is that it allows for more backing.

Leader to Fly Line

If the leader is coiled and stored in a package, remove it carefully. Place three or four fingers inside the leader coils and spread your fingers. With your other hand, carefully unravel the leader, butt section first, while maintaining finger

tension on the remaining coils until the leader is completely uncoiled. This simple procedure will prevent some time-consuming tangles. Now, using your hands, stretch and stroke the leader's butt section to remove some of the coil memory of the nylon. This makes tying it to the fly line much faster and easier. Put a simple, single overhand knot 2 or 3 inches from the butt end of the leader. This will ensure against a couple of errors that you might make as you attach the leader to the fly line.

Fly-Line Tip to Leader Butt match: (left to right) leader is too flexible = poor performance; leader and fly line are same stiffness = excellent performance; leader is stiffer than fly-line tip = poor performance.

For optimum casting performance, the fly-line tip and leader-butt junction should be of the same general flexibility. Good-quality leaders are usually designed with butts that match the fly-line tips. If your leader butt is too stiff, here's what to do to make it match: Stroke it with a smooth-jawed pair of needle-nose pliers to flatten the leader slightly. This will make the butt more flexible to match the fly-line tip.

Attach the leader butt to the fly-line tip by following the steps in the *Leader to Fly Line* illustration.

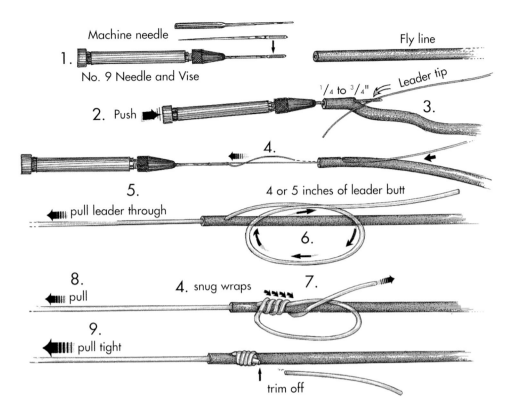

Machine needle

Fly line

1.

No. 9 Needle and Vise

$^1/_4$ to $^3/_4$" Leader tip

2. Push

3.

4.

5.

4 or 5 inches of leader butt

pull leader through

6.

8.

pull

4. snug wraps

7.

9.

pull tight

trim off

KNOT #3: DUNCAN LOOP—LEADER TO FLY LINE

Knot #3: Leader to Fly Line with Duncan Loop

This method works with knotless tapered leaders (with no tippet added yet) and braided hollow-core fly lines.

1. Begin with a size 8, 9, or 10 crewel or darning needle.

2. Insert the needle's eye end into the core of the fly line's tip $^1/_4$ to $^3/_8$ inch; then push it out the side of the coating, as shown.

3. Pass 1 inch of the leader tip through the eye of the needle. If the tip is too large, shave 1 or 2 inches of it with a razor blade until it is small enough to pass through the eye.

4. Pull the needle and end of the leader out of the tip of the fly line.

5. Pull the leader through the line tip to about 6 or 8 inches from the end of the butt.

6. With the end of the butt, form a loop next to the fly line, away from the tip end of the line.

7. Holding the leader butt loop and fly line firmly, make four snug, close-spaced wraps beginning at the exit hole, around the fly line

and through the loop as shown. Make sure that you wrap the leader butt *away* from the fly-line tip end.

8. Take great care to keep the leader-butt wraps tightly in place while pulling the leader in order to snug up the knot's wraps and loop.

9. Make one more extra-hard pull on the leader to snug it completely; then trim the excess leader-butt tag close to the knot. To make the knot smoother, coat it and the tip of the line with a fast-drying, flexible, waterproof cement, such as Zap-A-Gap or Dave's flexament.

NOTE: If you have a knotted tapered leader, follow these steps (and see diagram on page 33).

1A. Hold leader-butt end so that it curves up.

1B. Using a *new*, very sharp razor blade, stick the side of butt end at a 90-degree angle, 2 inches from the end. Then, change the angle to 10 degrees and slowly shave a portion away.

1C. Continue to rotate the butt and shave the end two or three times or until $1/2$ inch of end will pass through a size 8 or 9 darning-needle eye.

1D. Dull the needle point with a stone so it will pass easily inside the braided core of the fly line. Using a pin vise to hold the needle for steps 1D and 2A will help.

2A. Push needle point $1/4$ inch into the fly-line tip core and then out through the side of the line up to the needle eye. Place the leader butt through the eye $1/2$ inch and crimp.

2B. Pull the needle completely through the side of the line. Clear the leader from the eye, then *carefully* pull six to eight inches of the leader through the line tip. Then go to step 5 of the *Leader to Fly Line* instructions.

Other leader-to-fly-line options: If your line has a solid core, such as lead core, monofilament, Kevlar filament, or twisted filament, tie the leader to this with the Duncan Loop Knot #2 *(Backing to Fly Line)* method.

Note that two options besides the Duncan loop are included. One is a special Zap-A-Gap cemented leader-to-line connection that, when properly done, gives you a simple, smooth, and strong alternative. The other is a braided loop, which is popular for fast, loop-to-loop leader changing or because some folks do not wish to tie knots. There are also several gadgets for attaching the leader to

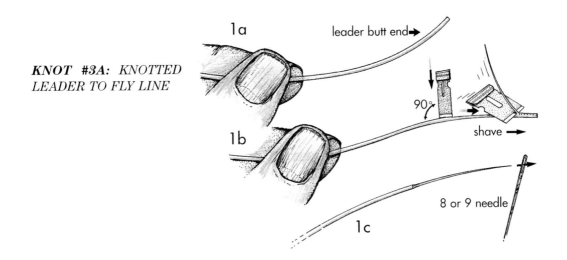

KNOT #3A: *KNOTTED LEADER TO FLY LINE*

1a

leader butt end→

90°

shave →

1b

8 or 9 needle

1c

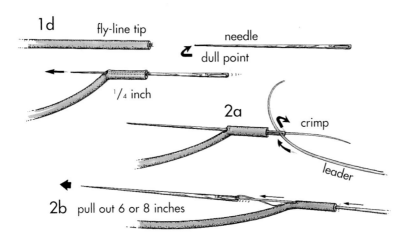

1d

fly-line tip

needle

dull point

¹/₄ inch

2a

crimp

leader

2b   pull out 6 or 8 inches

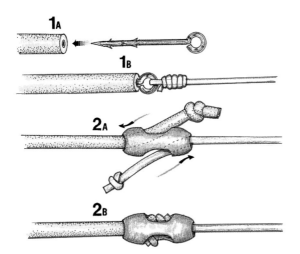

1A

1B

2A

2B

LEADER TO FLY LINE GADGET CONNECTORS

1A. *Insert the metal barbed eyelet into fly-line tip end.*

1B. *The leader butt is tied to eyelet with a clinch knot.*

2A. *Pass line and butt ends through connectors and form a simple single overhand knot in the end of each. Trim excess ends.*

2B. *Now pull both line and leader knots inside the connector.*

the fly line that I don't recommend. The metal eyelets with a barbed point and the plastic connectors are apt to fail. Besides, making the connections shown here takes about the same amount of time as installing the gadgets—and they are smaller, smoother, and much more dependable and efficient.

Zap-A-Gap Fly Line to Leader Connection, Option #1

Splicing the leader and fly line together with Zap-A-Gap is a no-knot option to using Knot #3. This glue has been thoroughly tested for superior waterproof bonding between nylon monofilament leaders and fly lines. Properly bonded, the fly line or leader butt will break before the connection fails.

1. Insert the eye of a size 8, 9, or 10 crewel or darning needle into the fly-line tip core. Use a pin vise to hold the needle.

2. Push the needle ½ inch up inside the fly-line core, then out the side of the coating.

3. Insert an inch of knotless leader tip (whose butt end has been straightened) through the needle eye.

4. Now pull the needle and leader tip out of the fly-line tip.

5. Remove the needle and pull the knotless leader, tip section first, through the fly-line tip until only 3 or 4 inches of butt remain outside of the needle hole.

6. Using 50- to 100-grit sandpaper, thoroughly roughen a ½-inch section of the leader butt next to the fly-line tip. NOTE: If leader-butt end has been straightened, the line/leader connection will also be straight.

7. Place a small drop of Zap-A-Gap on the roughened section and spread the glue evenly over it with the nozzle of the glue bottle. *Move immediately to the next step.*

8. Now quickly grip the exposed leader butt by the overhand knot with pliers or forceps and, holding the fly-line tip with a firm grip, give a quick, short pull on the leader-butt end to pull the roughed section just inside the fly line.

9. Allow fifteen to twenty seconds for the Zap-A-Gap glue to cure and form a permanent bond. Trim off the exposed excess butt end flush with the fly-line coating. After trimming, place a tiny amount

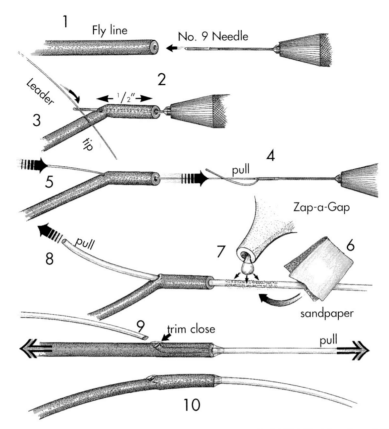

ZAP-A-GAP—LEADER TO LINE CONNECTION (Option #1)
(Designed by Joe Robinson of Austin, Texas.)

of Zap-A-Gap over the hole. Give a few sharp tugs on the leader butt and fly line to pull the end of the trimmed butt inside the fly-line core for a smooth surface finish.

NOTE: A small excess of glue may remain at the fly-line tip. If you allow this to dry for about thirty seconds it will provide a smoother link at the junction of fly line and leader butt. The glue drying may be accelerated to one second if you apply a catalyst called Zip Kicker. Zap-A-Gap is available through L.L. Bean as well as at fly-fishing, hardware, and hobby shops. It is distributed through Wapsi Fly Company, Route 5, Box 57 E, Mountain Home, AR 72653 and Umpqua Feather Merchants, P.O. Box 700, Glide, OR 97443.

The Speedy Nail Knot Connection, Option #2
The speedy nail knot is a fast option to attach a knotless leader or a leader-butt section to the fly line. It will not work on compound knotted leaders or braided-butt tapered leaders.

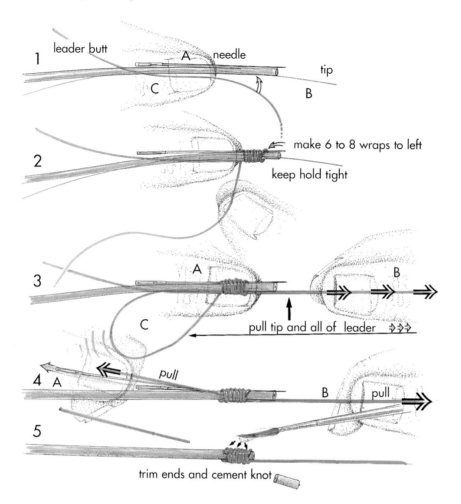

1   leader butt   A   needle   tip
    C   B

2   make 6 to 8 wraps to left
    keep hold tight

3   A   B
    C   pull tip and all of leader

4   A   pull   B   pull

5   trim ends and cement knot

SPEEDY NAIL KNOT—LEADER TO LINE CONNECTION (Option #2)

1A. With your left index finger and thumb, hold the fly-line tip and lay the point end of a small needle or toothpick next to the line tip.

1B. Place the leader tip next to the fly-line tip so that it extends 1 or 2 inches beyond the fly-line tip.

1C. Place the butt end of the leader next to the fly-line tip, with the butt end extending to the left past the needle eye 2 or 3 inches.

2. With your left index finger and thumb, grasp the fly line, needle, leader tip, and leader-butt firmly about 1 inch behind the fly-line tip end. With your right hand, wrap the leader butt section that is extending to the *right* of the left finger firmly over and around the fly line, needle, and leader butt and tip sections, 6 to 8 wraps,

1. Pull heat shrink connector onto the braid up to the loop.

2. Slip braid over the fly line by expanding braid.

3. Position the heat shrink connector half over the braid and half over the fly line. Carefully heat the connector with a match, lighter, or other heat source to just over 250 degrees Farenheit.

4. Connect line and leader butt with loop to loop connection. The leader loop is a double surgeon or prefection loop.

SLIP ON BRAIDED LOOP—LEADER TO LINE CONNECTION (Option #3)

progressively to the left. NOTE: The purpose of the needle is to give stiffness to make the wraps possible.

3A. Without letting the wraps loosen, slip your left finger and thumb carefully over the wraps and hold them in place with a firm squeeze.

3B. With your right finger and thumb, pull the leader-tip end to the right, until the entire leader (except the leader-butt tag) slides under the wraps.

3C. As you pull the leader through the wraps, be careful to keep the leader loop from twisting and tangling on itself or on your left hand.

4A. Continue holding the knot wraps firmly with your left hand. Using your right hand, pull on the tag end of the leader butt to tighten the wraps a bit more. Continue holding the knot wraps with your left hand and use your right hand to pull the needle to the left to remove it.

4B. With your right hand, pull on the leader tip to further tighten the wraps onto the fly line. When you are sure the wraps are tight, release the left-hand grip, and pull both the leader-butt tag and the leader-tip end to completely tighten the knot on to the fly-line tip.

5. Trim off the ends of the fly-line tip and the leader-butt tag. I'd advise also coating the fly line with a flexible, waterproof cement to make the knot and tip smoother so that the connection will pass through the rod guides more easily.

Tippet to Leader Tip

For connecting two sections of nylon monofilament line, whether for making a knotted tapered leader or tying tippet to tip, the *surgeon's knot* is superior to the popular blood or barrel knot. It is stronger, smaller, faster, and much easier to tie, and less sensitive to size or hardness mismatches. Practice this knot on level, 10- to 12-pound-test tippet material or scrap fly line before using it on your tapered leader tip.

It's good practice to add a tippet section to your new knotless tapered leader before you use it; about 18 inches is ideal. This addition only requires one small, dependable surgeon's knot, and it will significantly prolong your leader's life for two reasons. First, tying on flies uses up the inexpensive tippet rather than the expensive tapered leader; most knots use up 3 to 6 inches each time you change flies. Second, most leader damage, especially that due to abrasion or "wind knots," occurs on the 12 inches or so of your leader next to the fly. Your leader will last many times longer when you initially add a tippet.

Knot #4: Tippet to Leader Tip with Double Surgeon's Knot

1. Place leader tip and tippet section ends side by side in opposite directions, overlapping about 5 to 7 inches each.

2. With the lines together, twist and form a 2 inch-diameter common loop. Pass the leader-tip tag and the tippet's long end through the loop.

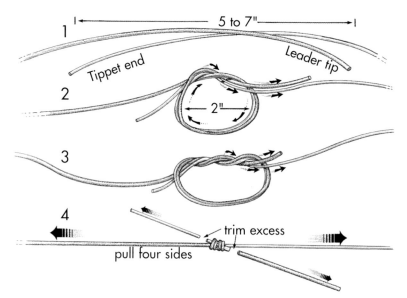

KNOT #4: DOUBLE SURGEON'S KNOT—TIPPET TO LEADER

3. Pass both through the loop once more. Wet the loop wraps with your lips.

4. Tighten the knot by first pulling on the long sides of leader and tippet, then on the tag ends. Trim excess tag ends.
   NOTE: If you are tying together two different types of nylon, it is best to make a third pass with both through the loop to prevent the harder type from cutting the softer type. For additional strength and efficiency, coat this knot with Zap-A-Gap.

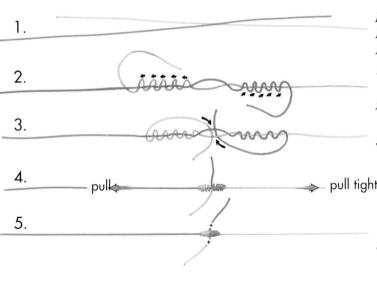

KNOT #4A: BLOOD KNOT (BARREL KNOT)—OPTIONAL TIPPET TO LEADER TIP KNOT

1. *Cross and parallel 6 to 8 inches of leader tip and tippet.*

2. *Take each tag end and wrap, or twist it four or five times around.*

3. *Now pass the tag ends through the loop that is between the two tippet wraps.*

4. *Wet wraps and pull both leader and tippet long ends apart smoothly to draw the knot wraps tight.*

5. *Test knot wraps with several sharp tugs. This also draws the knot down smaller and tighter. Clip tags close to knot. For superior performance and strength, lightly coat this knot with Zap-A-Gap.*

KNOT #4B: DOUBLE DUNCAN LOOP—OPTIONAL TIPPET TO LEADER KNOT

1a. *Place leader tip tag and tippet tag so that they cross each other with a 4- to 6-inch overlap.* 1b. *Form a loop with the tag end of the leader.*

2a. *With the leader tag end, form a three or four turn Duncan Loop knot onto the tippet section.*

2b. *Repeat 2a, using the tippet tag end.*

3a. *Wet and tighten each Duncan Loop*

3b. *Pull the leader and tippet in opposite directions to slide the two Duncan Loop knots together, firmly.*

4. *Pull tags tight, then cut away the tag ends close to the knots.*

Tippet End to Fly

Knot # 5: Tippet End or Leader Tip to Fly with Duncan Loop Knot

1. Pass 6 to 8 inches of the tippet's tag end through the eye of the hook.

2. First toward, then away from the fly, form a $1\frac{1}{2}$-inch-diameter loop with a tag.

3. Pass the tag through and around the loop and tippet five times; make sure the wraps are away from the fly.

4. Wet the wraps with your lips and snug the five wraps by holding onto the tag and pulling the fly as illustrated.

5. Tighten the knot by pulling very tightly on the tag end. The degree of tightening determines how easily the knot will slide on the tippet to form an open or closed loop. With a heavy tippet— over .011 inch—tighten the knot with pliers or hemostats.

6. Adjust the loop between fly and knot to the desired size for specific fly performance. Trim the excess tag.

This is a superb knot for tying all flies to your leader. It's fast and simple to tie and has excellent wet-knot strength. It can be tied in three configurations:

- A small open-loop knot for maximum fly action and good balance

- A larger loop knot for slip-shock absorption with heavy fish or rod strikes

- Tight against the hook eye to hold the leader hard against the fly

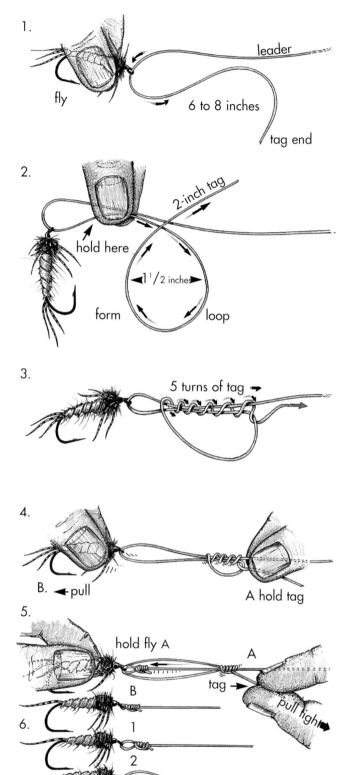

KNOT #5: DUNCAN LOOP—LEADER TIP OR TIPPET TO FLY

Duncan Loop options: (top to bottom) knot is pulled tight against hook eye; small loop to allow fly to move more naturally; large loop to increase strike shock absorption.

Duncan Loop Options

When properly tightened, a Duncan loop may be positioned to perform several options:

1. Clinched down tight next to the fly—for leader control of the fly's attitude.

2. Small open loop—to allow the fly to move more independently of the leader for more lifelike action, balance, and floating or sinking ability.

3. Large open loop—for shock absorption when the leader is violently or excessively strained by fish, obstruction, or angler.

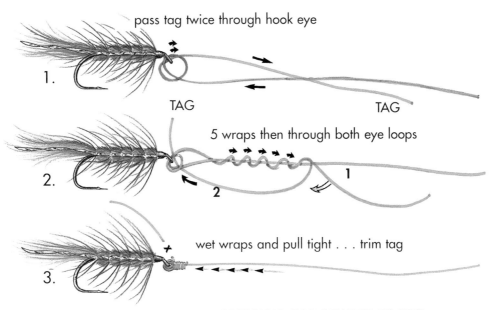

pass tag twice through hook eye

1.

TAG   TAG

5 wraps then through both eye loops

2.   1
    2

wet wraps and pull tight . . . trim tag

3.

KNOT #5A TRILENE KNOT—OPTIONAL FOR LEADER TO FLY

This is a good, strong knot and especially practical to tie on fly sizes 10 and larger.

1. *Pass the tag end of your tippet two times through the hook eye.*

2. *Make five wraps around the tippet with the tag, away from the hook. Bend the tag back toward the fly and pass it through both eye loops.*

3. *Wet the loops and wraps with your lips, then draw the knot down tightly by pulling on both the tag and the tippet. Cut away excess tag end.*

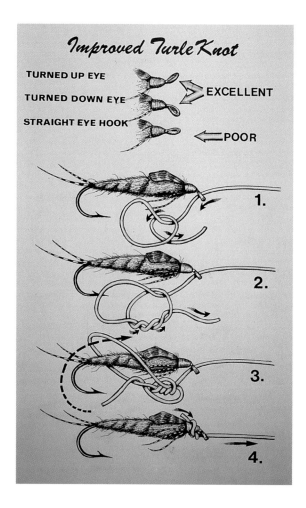

Improved Turle Knot

TURNED UP EYE

TURNED DOWN EYE ➤ EXCELLENT

STRAIGHT EYE HOOK ⬅ POOR

1.

2.

3.

4.

KNOT #5B: TURLE KNOT—
OPTIONAL LEADER TO FLY

This knot works nicely on turned-up or down eyed hooks but poorly on straight-eyed hooks. Use it when you want your fly to swim exactly in line with your leader tip.

1. *Pass 3 to 5 inches of the leader through the hook eye and form a loop with tag end.*

2. *Tie a double overhand knot at loop.*

3. *Pass loop over tail, hook, and fly body.*

4. *Snug loop tightly around fly head by pulling leader tight.*

Before attaching your fly, practice tying the Duncan loop with some excess 10- or 12-pound-test monofilament until you become proficient with it; also practice forming various loop sizes. The tighter the knot, the less the loop will slip shut or closed on the fly's eye. If properly tightened, it will not slip closed during normal casting or retrieving but will be easily opened with your fingernails if it slips closed on the strike or fight.

Practice all these recommended connections as many times as it takes for you to feel comfortable doing them quickly, neatly, and correctly. This investment will reward you with more fishing time and more success. Fly-line scraps or old fly lines make excellent, easy-to-see-and-handle practice materials. For this, you can cut 8 or 10 feet of fly line from the back of a weight-forward or level fly line without in any way hurting its practical length.

The Life of Fly-Line Components

Your backing should last for many years. The fly line will usually not need changing for at least two or three years of normal use and care. The leader, though, requires changing two or three times a season, more often if you fish a lot. The tippet may need replacing several times a day, and certainly each time you go fishing.

The fly needs to be replaced or retied regularly during a fishing day. The backing-to-fly-reel knot needs to be tied only once, backing-to-fly-line knot every two or three years, leader-to-fly-line knot three or four times a season, tippet knot two or three times a day, and fly knot about one to ten times each fishing day. That's why practicing the surgeon's knot and the Duncan loop many times is important. All knots tend to weaken when they become wet, or with use or age. Test all knots regularly and retie the tippet and fly knots regularly.

Wind Knots

Wind or overhand leader knots are tied unintentionally as you cast, due to either fishing accidents or casting faults. The most common cause is rushing or overpowering the casting stroke, trying to compensate for the wind's force against the cast—hence the name. Wind knots occur most frequently on the tip or tippet section of the leader. Though nearly invisible, they weaken the leader's strength by as much as 50 percent! This is because the overhand knot continues to tighten and cuts or squeezes itself when stressed. Wind knots must be removed. Those not yet tight can simply be untied. If a knot *is* tight, you must cut off the leader tip or tippet to the wind knot and either retie the fly at that point or replace the section removed with a new piece of tippet material using the double surgeon's knot, and then retie the fly to the new tippet. Wind knots occur less frequently on the heavier mid- or butt sections, but if they do, they may be untied or left there without severely weakening the leader. Check your leader frequently,

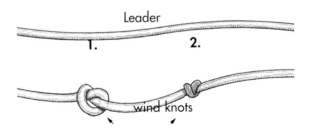

A knotless leader will be smooth if free of wind knots.

1. *A wind knot that has not yet tightened can be removed by untying it.*

2. *A wind knot that has tightened has already damaged and weakened the leader and should not be untied. Instead, the leader must be repaired or replaced.*

especially on windy days or if you notice the leader or fly-line tip striking or tangling with each other. In chapter 3 I will discuss how to prevent wind knots from occurring.

Droppers

At times you may wish to use two or more flies—called *droppers*—at once. Droppers are most easily attached simply by leaving a 4- to 6-inch-long tag on the leader-to-tippet surgeon's knot. Tie the dropper fly to the long tag with a Duncan loop or a trilene clinch knot.

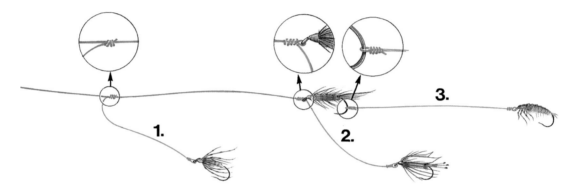

THREE TYPES OF DROPPER FLIES

1. *Use a Double Surgeon's knot to tie the tippet to the leader tip, then tie the dropper fly onto the tippet tag end.*

2. *With a Duncan loop or Trilene knot, tie the first fly onto the tippet. Using the tag end of the tippet, tie on the dropper fly.*

3. *Use a Duncan loop or Trilene knot to tie the dropper fly to the hook bend. Note: Dropper length may be from 6 to 18 inches. The shorter lengths tangle less on the leader and other flies.*

OPTIONAL KNOTS AND CONNECTIONS

I recommend the Duncan loop knot system for attaching four of the five major connections (Knots #1, 2, 3, and 5). For Knot #4 I recommend the simple, easy-to-tie, and highly efficient double surgeon's knot. However, L.L. Bean has asked me to include optional knots for connections #3, 4, and 5. Diagrams and directions for these follow:

| Knot #3 Options: | A–Zap-A-Gap connection | C–Braided loop |
| | B–Speedy nail knot | D–Double surgeon's loop |

Knot #4 Options: A–Blood knot (barrel knot)

B–Double Duncan loop

C–Improved Albright knot (for tippet to shock or bit tippet of heavy mono or wire)

Knot #5 Options: A–Trilene knot

B–Improved Turle knot

C–Improved clinch knot

D–Homer Rhode loop knot (for heavy bite tippet to fly)

Bite or Shock Tippet

Some freshwater and many saltwater predator fish have sharp, cutting teeth, fins, or gill plates that can cut your leader at the fly. To fish for these species without losing a lot of flies, you'll need to tie on a short tippet section of wire or extra-thick monofilament that will resist being severed.

Monofilament and metal bite tippets

For most of these bite tippet sections, 20- to 60-pound-test hard monofilament is ideal and preferred over the heavier and more kink prone wire tippets. Nylon bite tippets should be made from straightened, hard types of nylon monofilament such as Mason or Maxima.

The Albright knot is effective for these nylon-to-extra-heavy-nylon or nylon-to-wire connections. Here are instructions for tying an improved, slip-proof version of this popular knot.

BITE TIPPET

Some fish have sharp teeth and require a tippet that they cannot cut through.

1. Leader tip

2. Improved Albright knot—Leader to bite tippet

3. Heavy mason mono bite tippet (30 to 60 pounds)

4. Bite tippet to fly—Homer Rhode loop knot

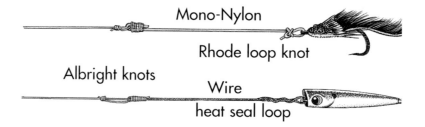

Two types of bite tippets: nylon and wire

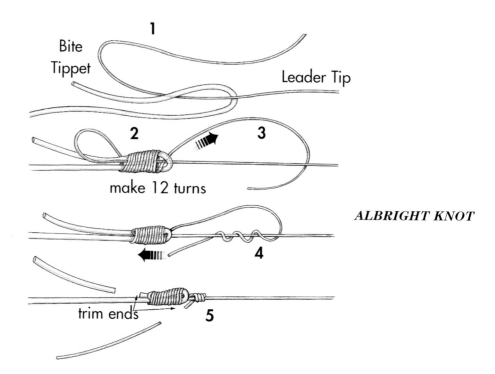

Improved Albright Knot for Bite Tippet

1. Form a short loop with bite tippet material and pass 8 to 10 inches of leader tip through the side loop.

2. Grasp and close the loop with your fingers and wrap the leader tip firmly and evenly around the loop end twelve times. Pass the leader tip through the loop as shown.

3. Pull the twelve wraps tight with the leader's end.

4. Wrap the leader's tip end around the leader three times and pass the tag end between the first wrap, then pull the wraps back tight against the bite tippet loop.

5. Tug on both sides of the knot to further tighten and test, then clip the excess ends. Coating this knot with Zap-A-Gap is highly recommended.

NOTE: If you are using a .012-inch or larger leader tip, you may need pliers to tighten the wraps.

To attach the fly to the nylon bite tippet, use a Homer Rhode loop knot. This knot provides a fixed open loop that allows the fly to move freely, even though it is tied to thick, stiff material. Note, however, that this knot is *not* used with normal-diameter tippet because it has only 50 percent knot strength.

Nylon Bite Tippet Fly Knot—Homer Rhode Loop Knot

1. Place a simple open overhand knot on the leader bite tippet about 3 to 6 inches from its tag end.

2. Pass the tag end through the eye of the hook.

3. Pass the tag end through the open overhand knot.

4. Snug down the overhand knot just in front of the hook eye as illustrated.

5. Take the tag end and pass it around the leader to . . .

6. . . . form a second snug overhand knot.

7. Work the second knot back to the first overhand knot. With pliers, pull the knot *very tightly* and trim off the excess tag .

NOTE: You can also use this loop knot for soft-braided wire tippet material if you tighten it correctly with pliers.

BITE TIPPET MATERIAL AND SIZE GUIDE (fresh and brackish water)

Smaller sizes of material are for smaller fish; the small size should be changed after you've caught one or two larger fish. *Chain Pickerel:* 20- to 30-pound monofilament. *Northern Pike*: 30- to 50-pound monofilament. *Muskie*: 40- to 60-pound monofilament or 15- to 20-pound braided wire. *Gar*: 15- to 25-pound braided wire. *Bowfish:* (grindle or dogfish) 30- to 40-pound monofilament or 15- to 20-pound braided wire. *Snook*: 30- to 60-pound monofilament. *Tarpon*: 30- to 80-pound monofilament or 15- to 30-pound braided wire. *Shark*: 15- to 30-pound solid wire. *Bluefish*: 30- to 60-pound monofilament or 15- to 30-pound solid wire.

Some fish can cut heavy hard nylon; for these you'll need braided wire coated with nylon. Attach the wire to the leader with the same improved Albright knot illustrated here.

To attach the fly to a nylon-coated braided wire, simply pass the wire through the fly's eye; twist it four to six times around itself and carefully heat the twists with a match flame or cigarette lighter until the nylon melts. Allow the wrap to cool and clip off the excess wire tag.

For other useful fly-fishing knots, I recommend Mark Sosin and Lefty Kreh's knot book, *Practical Fishing Knots.*

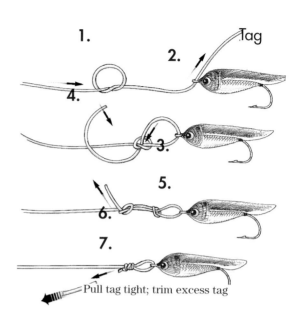

HOMER RHODE LOOP KNOT—NYLON BITE TIPPET TO FLY

Nylon-coated wire fly attachment. To seal wraps tight, carefully heat the wraps with a low flame.

ASSEMBLING FLY TACKLE FOR USE

Correct assembly of fly tackle can be simple and fast and will assure you of the best performance from your tackle.

Rod Assembly

Remove the fly rod from its protective tube and its cloth cover. Insert the rod's male ferrule into the female ferrule until you feel resistance. Align the guides on the different sections so they are in a straight line; you can adjust the alignment with a gentle twisting motion. Once the guides are aligned, apply a bit more push pressure to the ferrule to tighten the two pieces. Don't worry if the male ferrule seems a bit long; it is made this way to compensate for wear.

Fitting rod ferrules together. *Insert and twist to tighten. Make sure the line-up dots are even, or the rod guides are lined up straight.*

If the ferrules fit together loosely, take the rod apart and apply a thin film of beeswax or candle wax on the male ferrule; this will usually tighten up the fit without damage. If the ferrules feel gritty when you're putting them together, take them apart and clean them with soap and water. A cotton swab is excellent for cleaning inside the female ferrule.

Fly-Reel Attachment

Once the rod sections are together, attach the reel to the reel seat, making sure the spool handle is on your reeling hand's side. Finger-tighten the screw-locking ring. Rock the reel back and forth, then tighten the locking ring one more time.

Locate leader tip and pass it out of the reel spool's lower front area as shown.

Next, find the leader tip on the reel and pass it through the lower-forward position of the reel. Holding the rod handle, pull out the entire length of leader and one and a half times the rod length of fly line. Now place the reel-handle end of the rod on a clean, flat, nonabrasive surface (or have a companion hold it). If a clean surface is not available, place the rod handle and reel in your hat. Hold the rod near the ferrule and grasp the fly line 2 or 3 feet from the leader. Thread the doubled-over line through the guides toward the tip, taking care not to wrap the line around the rod between the guides. If possible, hold the fly rod guides-up when threading the lines. Pull the loose line and leader through the guides as you advance toward the tip. When you have 2 feet of fly line through the tip-top, release it and give the rod a couple of quick casting motions. The loose line between the reel and tip will quickly clear the rod tip.

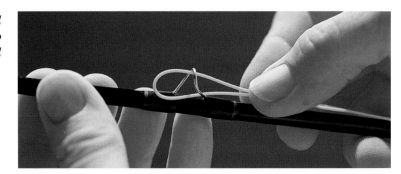

Double fly-line end and pass the loop through each rod guide.

Correct method for holding, warming, and straightening leader. Note that the leader and line are held very taut while the other hand strokes the tight area.

Leader Straightening

The leader and fly line will have developed a coil set from being stored on the reel spool. This set must be straightened for best performance. To do this, have someone hold the fly line near its tip or attach it to a door handle or other firm, smooth object. Stroke the leader with your hand until you feel it warm up. Hold the leader straight and tight for a few seconds as it cools to reset it in a straight condition. Repeat until most of the coils or kinks are removed. Your bare hand is a much better leader-straightener than commercial leather or rubber straighteners. They tend to "burn" the leader.

Fly-Line Straightening

A straight fly line, without reel-spool memory coils, will cast farther and more accurately than one with such coils. It will also float better and, without coil slack, will improve strike detection and hook-setting.

This waterline picture demonstrates how a straight fly line floats while an unstraightened one sinks.

Wrap fly line around a convenient, smooth object and then stretch and hold it for ten to twenty seconds. Slowly release the tension.

Over a clean surface, pull 30 to 50 feet of fly line off the reel. Have someone hold one end or attach it to a firm structure. Then pull the fly line tight until you feel it stretch just a bit. Hold it stretched for several seconds, *slowly* release tension, and see if the line has straightened. If it hasn't, repeat this procedure or stretch and gently stroke the line surface. A fly line is particularly difficult to straighten when the air is below 45 degrees F. When air or water temperatures are near or below freezing, the fly-line finish becomes hard. Under such conditions, the line can easily crack during stretching or fishing. To prevent cold-temperature cracking damage, avoid excessive stretching.

Fly to Leader

Now you are ready to tie on the fly, using one of the knots previously recommended. If you are just going to practice casting, you can tie on a practice fly—one with neither point nor barb.

When you assemble your tackle, be sure to place the empty cloth sack back in the fly-rod tube and put the lid back on the tube. This will ensure that the cloth sack does not get wet or dirty and that neither it nor the lid gets lost.

DISASSEMBLING FLY TACKLE

Proper disassembly of fly tackle is also important. It helps you prevent damage and ensures that the tackle will be ready the next time you need it.

When you stop fishing, reel in your line and make a few short, rapid false-casts to dry off the fly before removing it. Cut the fly from the tippet and place it in a hatband, on your fishing vest's fly patch, or in a well-ventilated fly box so it will dry completely.

To clean and dry your fly line immediately or shortly after use, lay it over the water or over a grit-free surface. With a clean cloth or paper towel in your rod hand, reel the fly line onto the reel spool while squeezing it with the towel. This removes most of the water and the dirty film that a line acquires during fishing. Always make sure when you reel the fly line onto the reel that it spools on firmly and evenly. Guide it with your rod hand, using moderate tension. Too-loose or uneven spooling may cause a bad tangle. If the fly line is wound on too tightly, however, it may kink or set in small loops or curls.

Leader Storage

As you wind the leader onto the fly reel, leave out about 4 to 6 inches of the tippet. This makes the fine tippet end much easier to find next time, and it also prevents the end from accidentally passing under the leader or line coils on the reel. If the leader does slip under the coil of line, it may form a half-hitch, causing a tangle and possible loss of a large fish. Pass the end of the leader out one of the reel-spool ventilation holes and back in another to keep it in place and prevent its getting lost in the spool.

Fly-Reel Storage

Remove the reel from the reel seat, wipe it clean, and dry it with a towel. If you have been fishing in brackish or salt water, be sure to wash the salt deposits off the reel and fly line with fresh water. Wipe dry, then allow to air-dry a few hours before storing. Place the reel in a well-ventilated bag or case to allow the damp fly line, backing, and internal parts of the reel to dry.

Disassembling Fly Rod

Now disassemble the rod. If the ferrules seem stuck, have a companion help you separate them—both of you should hold onto a different section of the rod and then pull slowly. Wipe the rod clean and dry with a towel. Replace it in the cloth rod bag and protective case. Be sure not to get the inside of the rod case or the rod bag wet. When storing, leave the lid off the tube until you are sure that the rod bag, the inside of the rod tube, and the fly rod are completely dry. It is essential that the rod and cloth bag be dry.

Store your tackle in a dark, cool, dry area. Proper storage prevents damage and premature aging.

Always disassemble the sections of your fly rod when storing it in a boat, car, or cabin, or when carrying it through dense foliage. Car doors, house doors, feet, and tree limbs are famous for their ability to break fly rods. Many more fly rods are broken as a result of carelessness than by fish or fishing.

With a clean rag, wipe your rod and reel clean and dry before storing them in their protective cases.

HOW TO FLY CAST

Casting well is the key to the successes and pleasures of fly fishing. You must devote more time to practice than you might for other casting methods, but your rewards will be many times greater. There is a poetic, hypnotic, almost sensuous feeling to casting a fly well. A good fly caster seems graceful and artistically endowed, and with practice you can feel this way, too!

▼

Learning to cast depends first on a clear understanding of the dynamics of propelling a *weightless* fly with the *linear* weight of the fly line using the *mechanical* control of the fly rod, your hand, your locked wrist, and your arm. To the casual observer—or even the experienced spin- and bait-casters—a fly caster appears to be simply waving the rod and line back and forth through a series of graceful arcs. *This is completely incorrect.* Fly casting is a precisely timed and controlled cycle of stroking motions that energize and direct the line and fly along an accurate path to the water.

First, you must focus on directing the *line*, not the fly! The leader and fly are pulled along with the line. Next, always keep in mind that the line is *linear* weight (weight that is spread over a long distance) under the control of your arm and hand through the fly rod. Unlike the case of other casting methods, the reel is not used during fly casting.

To move linear weight efficiently it must be *straight*. Consider a garden hose. If it's lying in loose coils on the ground, you can't move its whole length by holding one end and sweeping your arm. But if it's *straight* on the ground, you can move the entire length with a short sweep of your hand. This is the same principle that governs directing and moving a fly line.

The basic fly cast is performed with a length of fly line extended straight on the water in front of you. This is done in a four-part, continuous, timed sequence.

1. **Pickup**—Lifting the extended fly line up and off the water surface with the fly rod.

2. **Upstroke** (backcast)—Stroking the fly rod up and back by gradually accelerating and quickly stopping it to propel the lifted fly line, leader, and fly up and behind you—*straightening* the fly line for the next part of the cast.

3. **Downstroke** (forward cast)—Stroking the fly rod forward and down by gradually accelerating and quickly stopping it to straighten, direct, and deliver the fly line, leader, and fly toward the target.

4. **Presentation**—Directing the fly, leader, and fly line down to the water target area using the fly rod and gravity.

Study this casting procedure carefully to develop a strong visual concept of these crucial four parts.

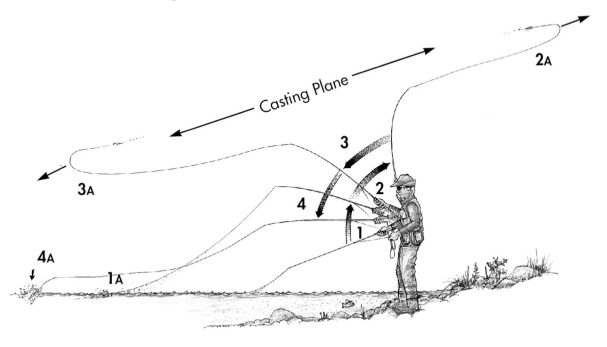

The four parts of a fly cast

The fly is not retrieved to the rod tip as is done in spinning and bait-casting with weighted lures. A fly cast must be started with at least 20 to 25 feet of fly line extended for there to be enough linear weight from the line to make the cast.

The path the fly line follows backward and forward is more or less straight and at a constant angle. This is called the **casting plane.** If the line does not travel in this *straight plane*, the cast becomes inefficient.

The direction the fly line travels is controlled by the stroking rod, hand, and arm. During the upstroke and downstroke, the fly rod is gradually accelerated and abruptly stopped at the end of each stroke. After the stop, the fly line continues to move in the direction of the stroke, and as it does, it forms a moving U-shaped *loop* that rolls over itself until the fly line, leader, and fly are fully extended.

Because the heavy, relatively stiff fly line always moves *with and in the same direction as the tip of the fly rod*, the loop shape and the line's direction of travel are under the fly caster's direct control. Precise control of the fly rod's movement means precise control of the fly cast, as if the rod tip were a pencil marking on paper.

The Four Parts of a Fly Cast

1. Pickup (lift).
1A. Start #2 when the leader begins to come off the surface.

2. The up-and-back casting stroke.
2A. Pause to allow the fly line, leader, and fly to unroll and straighten.

3. The down-and-forward casting stroke.
3A. Pause to allow the fly line, leader, and fly to unroll and straighten.

4. Presentation.
4A. Allow the fly, leader, and line to land on the water.

Loop control (both shape and direction) is the *key* to good fly casting. And the *path of the loop* (the casting plane) as it goes back and forth is the key to fly-casting efficiency and accuracy.

The four general loop shapes common to fly casting are *narrow, wide, open,* and *closed,* or *tailing.* These four loops and their many variations are direct results of timing and the arc that the rod tip follows during the power stroke. Or in other words, the moving rod tip forms the fly-line loop shape.

Which loop shape is correct? A narrow, or *tight*, loop is the most efficient for distance and best leader/fly delivery. The wide loop is less efficient because

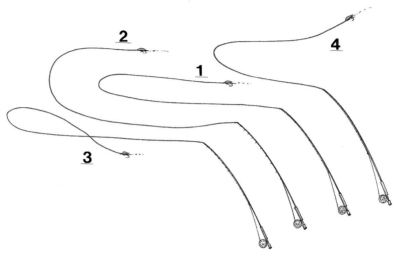

Four Loop Shapes
1. *Narrow loop*   3. *Closed or Tailing loop*
2. *Wide loop*   4. *Open loop*

it moves more slowly and has more wind resistance, but it may be useful for some fly presentations. The tailing and open loops are deformities caused by poor casting dynamics and are seldom if ever desirable.

The simplest way to understand and relate loop shape and control to the fly rod and casting stroke is to use what is known as the clock system. Visualize yourself standing with a large clock face at your side. The nine o'clock position is forward (the direction you are facing), twelve o'clock directly above your head, three o'clock behind you, and six o'clock at your feet. The fly rod is the clock hand.

To form a **narrow loop,** begin your cast with a pickup (lifting) motion from the water—eight o'clock lifting to ten o'clock.

For the up-and-back power stroke, gradually accelerate the rod from ten to twelve o'clock and quickly *stop there.* The tight loop then forms, moving in the direction of the stroke up and behind you and the rod tip stationary at twelve o'clock .

Just as the line, leader, and fly straighten out above and behind you (turn your head back and watch this), initiate your forward-and-down power stroke by *gradually accelerating* the fly rod from twelve o'clock to ten o'clock. *Abruptly stop the rod at ten o'clock!* This allows the narrow loop to form and move forward and down toward the target area. It's that simple.

If you had stroked from ten o'clock to three o'clock (waved your rod through a larger arc) and then from three o'clock back to ten o'clock, you would

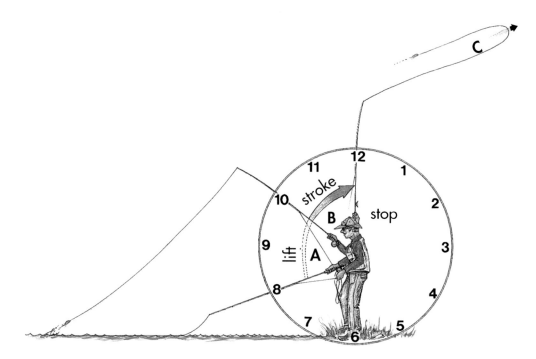

The Clock Method of four-part fly casting and loop shaping
A. Pick up: from 8 to 10 o'clock
B. Up-and-back stroke: from 10 to 12 o'clock and stop abruptly
C. The result is a narrow loop in the correct casting plane.

have had two very wide, inefficient loops. This would not have taken your fly as far or as precisely as the narrow loop. Unfortunately, many beginning fly casters have the rod-waving concept or have had experience with other casting methods using weighted lures and often fall into bad loop-shape habits—with frustrating results. It's human nature, if a loop is formed causing the fly to fall short, to *increase* the rod arc and try to force the fly line to go farther. *Less* arc and *less* power are the solution!

The closed, or tailing, loop is the most undesirable loop shape. It's caused when the caster either starts the forward stroke too soon (before the line straightens out in back) or accelerates the cast too fast at first. In either case, the flexible rod tip dips sharply down, or *shocks*, with the sudden overload of line weight and power, causing a portion of the line moving with the stroke to do so as well. This deformed, closed loop often catches on itself near the end of the cast, causing leader and fly tangles, overhand or wind knots, and poor presentations.

Remember that the movement of the rod tip forms the loop's shape. If the rod tip dips steeply and then straightens, that's what the fly line must do. Here's the solution: If you gradually and smoothly accelerate the stroke, the tip shock is far less likely to deform the loop shape.

The beginning fly fisher's most common error is to wave the rod, creating very wide or open loops. Using the wrist to move the rod up and back or down and forward is often the culprit. To prevent problems, keep your wrist more or less locked. As fly fishers become better casters, they sometimes begin to *force* the rod for extra distance and so develop tailing loops.

The degree of tip flex during the power stroke has a definite effect on loop shapes. Slow-action rods consistently form wider loops and more tailing loops than those with medium action. Medium-action rods often form loops a bit wider than those of fast-action rods. Medium-fast or fast-action fly rods are best for beginners for casting tighter, high-speed loops and are less prone to tip shock and tailing loops.

BASIC FLY-CASTING PROCEDURE

To learn the correct basics of fly casting as quickly as possible, I strongly advise you to *refrain from trying to catch fish* while you *practice* fly casting. Otherwise you will blur your focus on correct techniques, and may form bad casting habits. At our schools, we limit actual fishing until the students have practiced casting for *several* one- to two-hour sessions.

Before you begin, be sure that you understand the section on fly-casting dynamics. It's best to begin your fly-casting practice under the direction of a qualified instructor—preferably *not* a spouse or fly-fishing friend (who might cause unnecessary emotional pressure). If friends want to help, make sure that first they read and understand this section on fly-casting theory and method so they will speak the same language and not confuse you. It's better for you to understand this text and go it alone than to accept the help of an unqualified instructor. Learning any skill as complex as fly casting may be accomplished in several ways. The best way *for you* may differ from another's. Be aware of this and don't get upset when you discover varying teaching methods.

There are some fine videotapes on fly casting available, such as *L.L. Bean's Introduction to Fly Fishing*. If possible, watch it and others as you learn how to cast. (See the bibliography for additional instructional materials.)

Choose for your practice an uncongested, calm, *nonflowing* water surface such as a pond, lake, or swimming pool. The area should also have an unrestricted space of at least 40 feet behind you and 20 feet to either side. If such an area is unavailable, you might practice on a lawn or gymnasium floor. If you are casting over muddy, rough, or oily surfaces, spread out a plastic ground sheet or canvas to protect your fly line from damage and dirt. In any instance, try to practice when there is little or no wind. If you cannot escape the wind, try to position yourself so that it blows from your left side if you cast with your right arm, and vice versa.

It's important when practicing fly casting to use a small, hookless practice fly. Without a fly, the tackle does not cast correctly and this will misdirect your learning responses. To avoid accidents, use a fly that has had the hook point, barb, and bend removed; cut the hook off at the bend with a pair of pliers. Another option is to tie an inch or two of bright yarn or doubled pipe cleaner to the leader tip. Now straighten your leader and about 40 feet of fly line as described in chapter 2.

Hold the rod in your casting hand (your writing hand) and strip about 30 feet of line off the reel with your other hand. Let this line fall to the ground at your feet. Grasp the fly and leader and pull about 25 feet of fly line out through the tip-top. Lay this line on the ground in a straight line behind you to its full length, including the leader.

Facing the direction in which you intend to cast, place your feet about 1$\frac{1}{2}$ feet apart and move your casting-arm foot a bit behind the other. If you are casting over water, stand at about water level and only a foot or two from the edge; be sure the area is clean so that the excess line does not tangle or become dirty. By positioning your feet as recommended, you will be standing slightly sideways of the direction in which you intend to cast. This stance is necessary to allow you to watch both your up cast and down cast unroll. *You cannot learn to fly cast well if you do not observe* both *your backward and forward casts.*

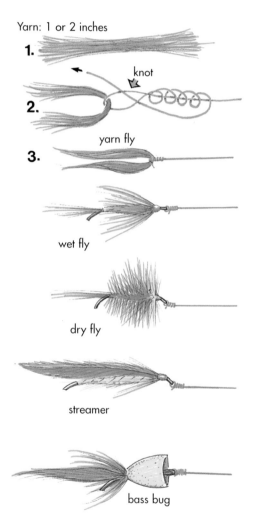

Yarn: 1 or 2 inches

1.

knot

2.

yarn fly

3.

wet fly

dry fly

streamer

bass bug

Five examples of highly visible, hookless practice flies. Try to match fly type and size to tackle and fish flies on or near the surface for best practice.

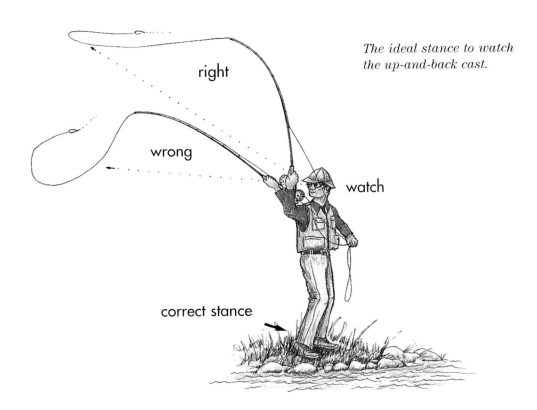

right

wrong

watch

correct stance

*The ideal stance to watch
the up-and-back cast.*

Hold the rod, reel, and line as shown in the accompanying illustration. Make sure that your thumb is on top of the rod handle and that you have positioned your grip on the handle comfortably. Avoid placing your index finger on the top of the handle, for this position will not give you the stability you need. Likewise, avoid placing your thumb on the side of the handle—this splits your control, and you do not want the rod to twist or rotate in your grip. Hold the fly line between the reel and the first stripper guide with your other hand to maintain line control.

The hand that holds the fly line while you cast and fish may be thought of as your reel hand. It performs many fly and fly-line control functions; at first, however, simply teach it to hold the line tightly between the reel and the first rod guide. (Study the photo.) If you release your grip on the fly line during the cast, the slack line will cause casting problems.

Before starting to cast, take a few slow, deep breaths and relax. With the fly rod in about the one o'clock position, cast forward, putting the fly in front of you in the water or grass. The fly line should be extended more or less straight on the area in front of you! Now begin to make the four parts of a fly cast—pickup, up-and-back cast, down-and-forward cast, and presentation.

Correct grip on fly-rod handle to fly cast. Thumb on top and four fingers wrapped around lower side of handle.

Alternative grip: Some fly-fishing instructors recommend placing the index finger on top of the rod, thumb to the side, and three fingers beneath the handle.

Incorrect grip for fly casting: This grip gives you minimal rod control and is very tiring.

Reel hand holds fly line firmly as line is cast with rod hand.

Pickup (Lift)

With the rod tip straight forward and almost touching the water or ground (about eight o'clock), begin to lift your fly rod in a smooth, steady motion, raising your arm and fly rod, lifting the fly line off the water. This pickup motion should be slightly off the side of your casting shoulder and upward. Keep your *wrist locked* to avoid any rod-tip rotation as you lift with the rod and arm; resist the tendency to "rip" the fly line off the water with a nervous jerk. When all but the leader and fly are off the water, the rod angle should be somewhere around ten o'clock. Your line hand and arm should be held *slightly* forward and low, and kept relaxed through all four parts.

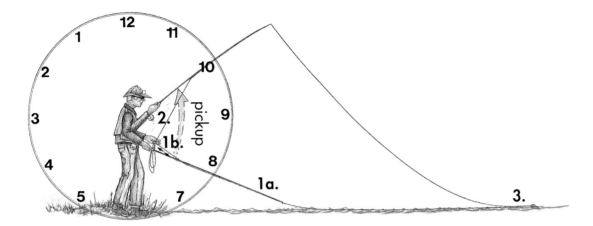

PICK-UP METHOD to Begin Cast

1a.   *Begin pickup with rod tip almost touching the water's surface and pointing toward the fly.*

1b.   *With the fly-line hand, pull any slack out of the fly line between your hand and the fly.*

2.   *Immediately after step 1b, begin to pick up the fly line from the water with a smooth, steady rod-lifting motion. Try to use your height and arm length to raise the line up into the casting plane rather than rotating the fly rod to a high angle. Study this diagram carefully.*

3.   *Watch your fly-line tip/leader/fly area and try to pick up the line to at least this point; then, without pausing, allow the fly to leave the water smoothly to start your up-and-back cast so that the line and rod angle are in the best casting-plane position.*

Note: The clock is reversed to show the casting arm movements of a right-handed caster.

Up-and-Back Cast

Without pausing after the pickup, begin the up-and-back motion using mostly your forearm and locked wrist. You want to gradually accelerate the rod from ten o'clock to eleven o'clock to make sure the line is all straightened in front of you; this is often called *loading the rod*. Then between eleven o'clock and twelve o'clock, apply the faster, power portion of the stroke using the energy needed, say, to toss a golf ball that high and far behind you. To create a good, tight loop, you must stop the rod abruptly at twelve o'clock. Focus your stroke energy on your index finger's pressure on the underside of the rod's handle. You're trying to cast the fly line up and over yourself from off the water so that it will *straighten* out above and behind you. During initial practices, *you must watch the fly line* to do so! This way you can see whether you have stopped at the right clock position and whether you have given the stroke enough power;

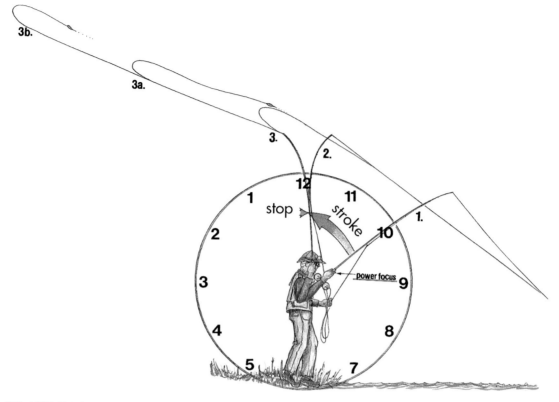

UP-AND-BACK CAST

1. *Begin stroke with a slow, smooth acceleration from approximately 10 to 11 o'clock.*

2. *Stroke from 11 to 12 o'clock with maximum power and acceleration.*

3. *Stop stroke abruptly at 12 o'clock. This causes a loop to immediately begin to form and move up and back past rod tip.*

3a. *Narrow loop unrolls up-and-back.*

3b. *Up-and-back cast complete and forward- and-down cast should begin.*

you will then know precisely when to start the third phase, which is just *before* the leader and fly come straight back and begin to fall. Eventually, watching your up-and-back cast will not be necessary.

If you stand correctly, you can comfortably watch your up-and-back cast. This is an absolute must if you want to develop a correct and well-timed up-and-back cast and a precisely timed down-and-forward cast stroke. The trick to watching the up-and-back cast is to turn your head just before or as you start the pickup and quickly focus on the area where you want your up-and-back cast to end up. Don't try to focus and follow the cast as it leaves the water and moves past and behind you; your vision will usually blur, causing disorientation and discomfort. It helps to have the backcast area in shadow and free from glare.

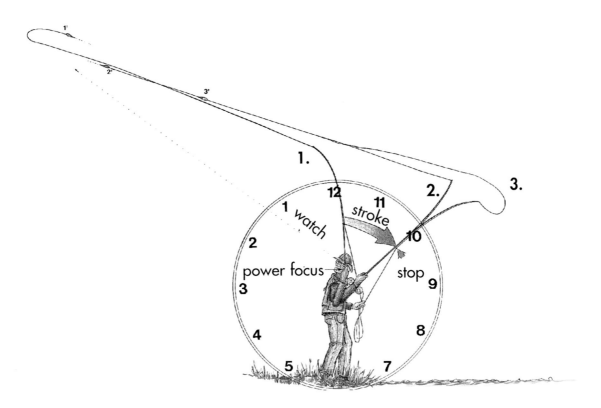

FORWARD-AND-DOWN CAST

1. *You should be watching your fly, leader, and line tip. Just before they straighten, slowly begin a smooth stroke forward from 12 to 11 o'clock.*

2. *Stroke from 11 to 10 o'clock with maximum power and acceleration then stop abruptly at 10 o'clock*

3. *The forward-and-down stroke and stop forms the loop shape and determines the direction it will travel.*

Down-and-Forward Cast

With your fly-rod tip at about twelve o'clock and as the fly line straightens out above and behind you, begin a slowly accelerating down-and-forward stroke, using mostly your forearm and locked wrist. You'll drift forward and down, slowly accelerating from twelve o'clock to eleven o'clock to ensure that the line is completely straightened out behind you (loading the rod) and to prevent shocking the tip. Next, apply the faster, power portion of the stroke between eleven o'clock and ten o'clock. Just as you focused your energy on the index finger for the up-and-back cast, focus the down-and-forward stroke energy on your thumb's pressure on the top of the rod's handle! Stop the rod motion abruptly at ten o'clock, *keeping the tip high at ten o'clock,* and watch the fly-line loop form and move forward past the rod and toward the water or ground.

Presentation

As the fly line, leader, and fly reach the extent of their length forward, begin to follow the falling line with your fly-rod tip down to around eight o'clock, until the fly line and fly rest on the water.

Repeat this four-part procedure for three to five minutes to get the feel of your tackle and casting. Stay relaxed and loose; don't hold your breath or rush the casting cycles. If your back or forward casts are weak or falling short, increase your stroke power. Remember, overcoming the water's hold on the fly and over-coming gravity during the up-and-back cast takes *more power* than casting that same load downhill with gravity during the down-and-forward cast. Most beginning fly casters tend to reverse these power needs. Especially concentrate during your practice on keeping the ten o'clock to twelve o'clock arc in your back-and-forward casts to assure a good loop shape and *correct casting plane.*

The overhead or over-shoulder casting position is the best to begin with since it relates easily to the clock method. But as soon as you have a clear understanding of the clock and of loop shapes and casting planes, it's easier to practice casting with an off-shoulder position. This is because your arm and shoulder muscles and reflexes are more comfortable and familiar with making off-shoulder or sideways strokes—with baseball bats, tennis rackets, and the like. Also, sidearmed, your fly line will travel a bit lower and more to the side,

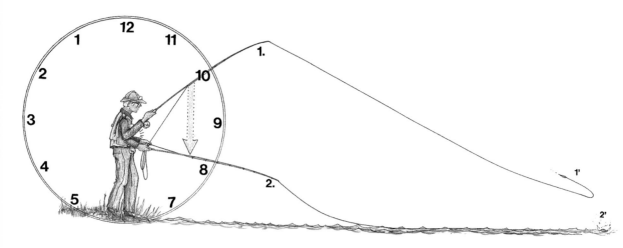

PRESENTATION

1. *Keep rod at 10 o'clock until loop completely unrolls and the fly is near one foot from the water.*

2. *When the fly settles on the water (2 feet) lower rod to whatever position is required to either make the next pickup or fish the fly.*

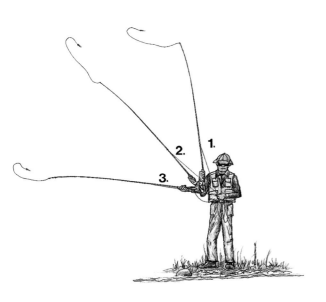

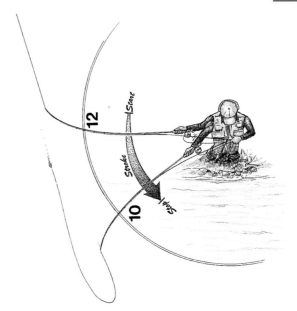

This front view of a fly caster shows the three main casting angles.

1. *Overhead or shoulder cast*
2. *Off-shoulder cast*
3. *Side-arm cast*

SIDE-ARM CAST CLOCK
For correct side-arm casting, visualize a horizontal clock. Angle the casting arm to the side and follow the same procedure as with overhead casting.

making it easier to watch your backcast and rod-tip position than when casting overhead. This cast angle also helps prevent the fly and fly line from striking the rod or you accidentally. Study the off-shoulder and sidearm casting diagram carefully.

When you actually fly cast for fish, you will use some form of sidearm position for most of your casts. This lower-angle cast is less hazardous, less affected by wind, and less visible to fish. But don't forget the clock angle; just imagine it tilted over at the same plane as the fly rod moving at your side.

As you get some feel for casting, let's add further suggestions. Place a hula hoop or dishpan on the surface to serve as a target. Look at this target as you begin each forward-and-down stroke, and make that stroke toward the target. It's not necessary to *hit* the target, but trying to will motivate you and develop your aim. Adjust your casting plane so that the loop travels straight toward the target and so that the fly strikes the target area just as the leader turns it over. Most fly presentations require the fly to either strike the target area directly or fall from 1 to 2 feet above it for a softer, more delicate landing.

To hit the target area with your fly, adjust the casting plane so that the fly travels in a more or less straight path to the target. Note that just as the fly and the leader straighten forward, the fly strikes the target area.

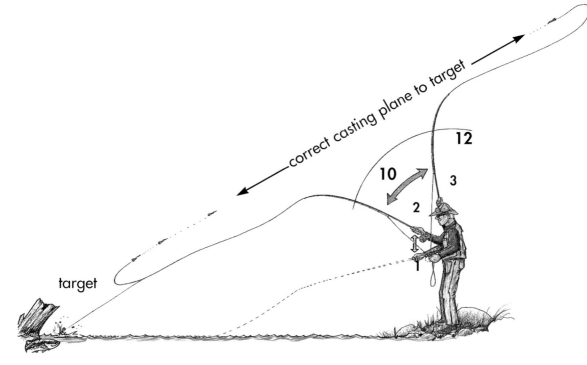

Practice to a target to obtain accuracy.

1. Pickup begins at eight o'clock to about ten o'clock; this is the beginning point of the casting-plane angle needed to hit the target.

2. Up-and-back stroke from ten o'clock to twelve o'clock so that the fly and line travel in the correct plane.

3. The down-and-forward stroke from twelve o'clock to ten o'clock puts the fly on target. Now lower your rod back to the first position in order to fish the fly.

If the fly and the line strike the water in a splashy pile short of the target, you're most likely bringing the rod tip too far down, perhaps to nine o'clock or eight o'clock, thus creating a "wide" loop and not allowing the fly line to extend to the target. Remember: *The fly line always follows the direction of the rod tip.*

If your line and fly go out high over the target and fall back toward you in a messy heap of fly, leader, and line tip, this is because your down-and-forward rod stroke is actually more forward-and-*up* and is ending too high ("high stroking"). This causes the fly line, leader, and fly to straighten out at a high angle; the leader and fly are then pulled back toward the rod tip by the falling line's weight. Most likely this high stroking is caused by your allowing the rod,

CASTING PROBLEM: Line, leader, and fly splash in a pile on the water. Rod is being stroked to the 9 or 8 o'clock position. Stop and hold rod at 10 o'clock until line rolls out and fly touches the water.

CASTING PROBLEM: Line straightens forward too high and falls down and back into a pile. The forward-and-down stroke is angled too high (going forward-and-up).

during the up-and-back cast, to go too far back and down, to the two, three, or four o'clock position. This causes a change in the casting plane from ten/twelve/ten o'clock to ten/two/twelve o'clock. This is the most common fly-casting error.

FALSE-CASTING

After you've learned the four parts of the cast, it's time to try some false-casting.

False-casting is merely eliminating the presentation and pickup sequences for one or more casts while repeating the up-and-back and down-and-forward parts continuously. False-casting is used to extend fly-line length, to hold the fly in the air above the water until you pick a target, to change fly-line direction, or to remove water from a soggy floating fly. False-casting is also useful when practicing your loop control and fly-casting technique. When you are fishing, however, too much false-casting can cause fatigue and poor timing, as well as frighten fish. If you false-cast sparingly, it will serve you well.

To false-cast, eliminate the presentation part of the four-part cast, and as the line straightens forward above the water start another up-and-back cast. Don't let the fly hit the water, and in a back-and-forth casting cycle hold the fly up in the air. At first, using a short length of fly line (20 to 30 feet), practice doing just one false-cast; then do two or three. False-casting can be tiring, so don't over-practice until you've built up your endurance.

As you practice, at this point resist the temptation to extend the fly-line length! Stay within about 20 or 30 feet or a length you feel comfortable using. Choosing a fixed target at a fixed distance will help you avoid the temptation. Using too much line will cause problems with timing, loop control, casting plane, presentation, and fatigue, and this will discourage you. Most of my fly fishing is done at 30 to 40 feet; longer distances are seldom required and are usually not as productive. In time, however, and with correct technique, you will be able to achieve much longer casting distances with ease.

Good fly casting is not based on strength but on proper timing and correct technique. Expert fly casters appear

THE PERFECT FLY CAST
To make a perfect fly cast, each of these four steps must be accomplished correctly. It's natural for you to emphasize the down-and-forward cast most. But the single most important part of the cast is the pickup. If this is not correct, it is impossible to proceed with a perfect cast. This may surprise you, but there are relative values for each part of the cast:
1. Pickup—50 percent
2. Up-and-back cast—25 percent
3. Down-and-forward cast—15 percent
4. Presentation—10 percent
In our years at the L.L. Bean Fly-Fishing Schools, we have found that practically every incorrect casting habit or problem can be directly traced to an incorrect pickup.

to make long casts effortlessly. This is because they do not throw the fly line with their arm speed but correctly energize (or load) and stroke the fly rod and then allow *it* to unflex and cast the fly line. Because many of us have used our arm's speed (as a short lever) to throw balls or rocks, we tend to try to throw the fly line and rod with arm speed as well. This is a mistake. Just use your shoulder, arm, wrist, and hand torque to energize the rod through the smooth, accelerating casting stroke. The fly rod is a fine casting tool that gives you so much leverage you need only a small amount of strength to fly cast. That's why you can fly fish effectively from age nine to ninety (and longer).

ROLL-CASTING

Roll-casting is a forward cast without a backcast. Some fly-fishing instructors prefer to teach the roll-cast first; I believe either order works nicely. It uses the same fly-casting dynamics and, like the false-cast, merely modifies the basic four-part cast.

The roll cast must be practiced over water, never on dry surfaces. See illustration at bottom of page.

Pickup

This is the most important part. With the fly line extended forward on the water and your rod tip pointed low and toward the fly line, begin a slow arm- and rod-

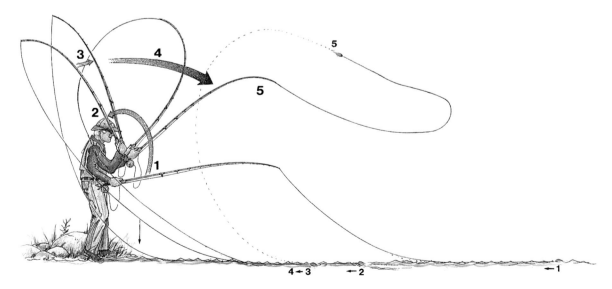

ROLL CAST

lifting motion that ends with your arm extended up and to the side, with the rod tip pointing at two o'clock. Do not rush; pause a second or two. This pickup motion should slide the fly line, leader, and fly on the water toward and slightly to your side (the off-shoulder rod position). Do this pickup motion in slow motion. With the pause to the two o'clock position, the fly line you have lifted off the water will sag down beside and behind your shoulder.

Down-and-Forward Cast

After the pause, move your fly rod to the twelve o'clock position. From there begin the basic down-and-forward power stroke toward the target. Stop the tip abruptly at ten o'clock. There is a temptation at this point to lower or stroke the tip down too far, even striking the water with it. Don't let this happen or the fly line, leader, and fly will simply pile up on the water somewhere between the rod tip and target. You need to make a basic forward cast so that the fly-line loop will form and move forward with leader and fly. If the forward-rolling loop and fly fall short of straightening out, increase the power of your stroke and check that you are stopping your rod tip abruptly at ten o'clock.

Presentation

As the loop unrolls forward, the leader and fly follow it as the line falls to the water; after the fly and leader hit the water, follow the line down with the rod tip to the eight o'clock position. That is a completed roll-cast.

Repeat this procedure a number of times. Because it's so important, once again I'll remind you: Don't rush the pickup. Don't accelerate the down-and-forward cast too abruptly, making the rod-tip arc go only from twelve o'clock to ten o'clock. Practice the roll-cast until you feel confident with it, then try it in the sidearm and backhand casting positions.

The roll-cast works without a backcast because it places the fly-line weight behind you with the two o'clock rod-angle pickup and pause. This pulls the remaining line and fly up and forward off the water, as the forward-moving loop passes over them. However, it is not a long cast—usually 20 to 40 feet, seldom over 50 feet.

The roll-cast has almost unlimited uses in fly fishing. Here are some of its most important:

- When an obstacle is above or behind you, you can still make a forward cast without snagging your fly.

- It's the perfect method for picking up or straightening slack fly line.

- A modified roll-cast allows you to swim a fly in any direction on the water.

- It makes lifting and pickup of a sinking-tip or full-sinking fly line easier.

- It aids in unhooking your fly when snagged on an obstacle.

- To make a slow, delicate fly presentation.

- To assist in hook setting when excess fly-line slack is unavoidable.

- For repositioning your fly line if it should blow or drift too far to your side for safe or correct pickup.

- For making an easier down-and-forward cast when there is a strong wind at your back.

- For reaching your fly—to inspect or change it—without reeling or stripping in your fly line.

THE FLY-LINE HAND

As you hold the fly rod to cast, fish, hook, and fight fish, your other hand is in constant use, too. Let's add this hand into our casting practice. The fly fisher uses the fly-line hand on each cast to tighten the fly line on pickup, to extend more fly line when casting for extra distance, and to retrieve and animate the fly. If a fish strikes, the fly-line hand helps set the hook, control the line and fly reel throughout the battle, then, with net or bare hand, land the fish. Clearly the fly-line hand has a key role in fly fishing.

Before you begin your pickup, with the fly-rod tip at its lowest angle, use your line hand to remove any slack from the line. This simple tightening of the fly line will ensure a much more efficient pickup, and in turn a much better cast.

As you lift the line off the water with your rod and casting arm, hold the fly line tightly in your line-hand thumb and first finger, keeping your line hand and arm stationary. Better yet, use your line hand to make a short downward pull, or *haul*, just as you begin the up-and-back stroke. This simple technique will increase line speed, which helps move it off the water and upward, improving pickup efficiency.

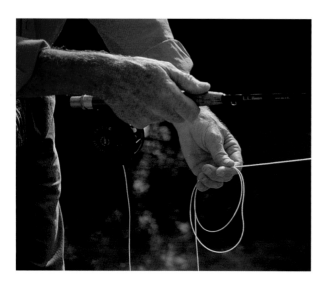

Shooting out extra line

Step 1: Hold extra line in your reel hand.

Step 2: When forward-and-down casting stroke is completed and line moves forward, relax your grip on the line coils and let them be pulled out by the extended forward moving line.

Using the Line Hand for Extra Distance

To cast farther, add extra power to the down-and-forward stroke. As the over-accelerated line and fly move well forward of the rod tip, you should feel a slight line *tug* on your line hand. As this occurs, loosen your finger hold on the fly line, and the extended line weight will pull out more line from your hand proportional to its excess energy. This is called **shooting line.** For maximum effect, the line hand must be trained to sense this pull and release the line at precisely the right time. When you first try this, you will probably release the fly line *during the power stroke,* which will add slack and spoil the cast, actually reducing your distance. Delay the line release; watch the line move forward until you *feel* the tug.

When adding extra power to the down-and-forward stroke, you must still accelerate slowly and smoothly and maintain the rod-tip stop position at ten o'clock. If the rod goes lower on the stroke, you'll force the fly line to dive steeply at the water rather than unroll over it; this shortens rather than lengthens the cast. Remember to watch the fly line move well forward. As it does, if you've given the cast enough extra power, you'll feel the fly line tug and release properly for the shoot. The more line you have extended, the better. Shooting line works because more weight pulls out more line.

NOTE: Never turn the fly line completely loose from your line hand's control as you cast and shoot fly line. Release the finger hold into a circle formed with your thumb and index finger. (See photograph.)

Establishing Absolute Line-Hand Control

As your fly nears the water, you should have control over it. This is done by establishing a **two-point** (two-hand) hold on the fly line. This allows you to control precisely the tension on the fly line for animating the fly, retrieving it, detecting strikes, hooking fish, and manually pulling the fish to you. *Mastering this two-point method is an absolute must for successful fly fishing.* Here's how to do it:

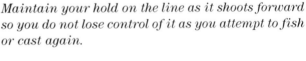

Maintain your hold on the line as it shoots forward so you do not lose control of it as you attempt to fish or cast again.

1. As the fly line, leader, and fly start to fall to the surface, begin to move your line hand toward your extended rod hand. Keep your eyes on the fly.

2. Extend the first or index finger of your rod hand down from its grip on the rod handle.

3. With your line hand's fingers, make direct contact with your rod hand's extended finger, placing the fly line across the extended finger. Now grasp the line with the rod hand's index finger and press it against the rod handle. Do not release your line hand's grip on the fly line. Now you are controlling the line in a two-handed hold.

4. With this two-point method, you have the best possible control on the line and fly for controlling initial slack and tension, animating and retrieving the fly, feeling the strike, setting the hook on a strike, and controlling slack and tension on the line as a hooked fish fights.

   If you have spin-fished, an excellent way to understand this two-point control system is to consider the rod-hand index finger's grip on

One-point line control position for casting, hauling, and shooting fly line.

Two-point control position for retrieving fly line,
setting the hook, and fighting a fish.

the fly line as the bail of a spinning reel, and the line-hand grip as the spinning-reel handle. If you fail to close the bail or engage the handle, you have no line or lure control. That is what happens when you do not use fly fishing's two-point system.

5. Just as you begin the pickup for the next cast, release the rod hand's finger hold on the fly line.

A caution: As you initially practice two-point control, you will probably try to steer the fly line onto the rod finger by reaching with the rod hand (and fly rod) for the fly line. You'll quickly see that this doesn't work well. The *line hand* must move *to* the rod finger while keeping the fly rod in the correct fishing position.

Each time you cast and present the fly, establish your two-point control. Retrieve the fly by making a few short line strips with your line hand. Relax your rod-finger grip tension each time you pull on the line with your line hand. Then, as you reach for additional lengths of line *just behind your rod finger,* tighten your rod-finger grip so as not to allow the fly line to become slack. Always reach for more fly line *behind the hand.* Practice this with every cast until it is automatic. This is because you will need two-point control every time you fish a fly.

You can use two-point control to fight and pull in a small fish, but it's usually best to eliminate the excess line that accumulates between your hand and the

To put fish "on the reel," use the two-point control hold while using your little finger to keep slack line tight as you reel it on to the reel spool.

Correct hand position to fight fish directly off reel.

reel. To prevent tangling, after you set the hook and have the fish under initial control, place the slack line in your rod hand's small finger and begin winding the line onto the reel, using the small finger to provide tension and level-winding control for the spooling fly line. Make sure you have the fish *well hooked* and under *tight line* control before you attempt to reel up the slack fly line, then reel it up smoothly so that the fly rod's tip doesn't jiggle and possibly dislodge the hook from the fish's mouth.

Once all this slack is on the fly reel, release the rod finger's grip on the line. Now you can fight the fish from the reel, using cranking speed and your rod to control slack and line tension until the fish tires and is landed.

This may seem obvious to some, but others seem to miss this point: Most of the fly's movements on the water are the result of line-hand pulls and rod-tip movements. As you pull, you are shortening the amount of fly line you have extended. Try at this point to keep at least 20 feet of line extended to provide enough casting weight for the next cast. Then, as you make the next cast and want to extend the line and fly out farther, do so by overpowering and shooting out extra line, as explained earlier. One or more false-casts may be necessary to extend the fly line longer distances. As you practice, try to work on each of these procedures.

OTHER CASTING TECHNIQUES

Besides basic casting and roll-casting, there are other techniques that you will want to master to fully enjoy fly fishing.

Shooting line is similar in purpose to working out line. As mentioned earlier, it is accomplished in either the backward or forward cast by using considerably more power than is needed to cast the line already extended. In either the backward or forward cast, slack line is fed out just as the moving loop reaches its end, thus pulling or shooting the extra slack out with it. The weight-forward taper is best for shooting out extra line. Generally, shooting out line reduces the number of false-casts needed and adds casting distance.

Hauling is a technique for increasing line speed or overall fly-casting efficiency by using the power of both the rod arm and the line-hand arm. To accomplish a haul, the caster, just as the power stroke is applied with the fly rod, simultaneously pulls down, with the line hand, on the taut fly line below the first stripper guide. This pull—or haul—increases the line's forward or backward speed. **Double-hauling** involves hauling on both the forward and backward strokes.

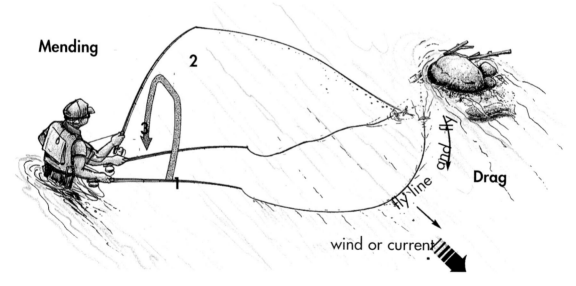

Mending is used to compensate for unwanted line drag which is caused by flowing water or surface wind.

1. *When unwanted drag begins to develop, lift the section of fly line causing drag off the water.*
2. *Using the rod, place the fly line in the opposite direction of the drag.*
3. *Rod back into fishing position.*

Hauling should not be attempted until you have mastered loop control. Only then does it become a useful method for better line pickup and for making long, powerful casts. If you try hauling before you have mastered loop control, it will have an adverse effect on your overall casting ability.

Mending line is an extremely important technique for repositioning the line and leader on moving water to better control the fly. Mending is accomplished by using various rod-lifting and roll-casting rod movements. When you are fishing streams, mending line is about as important as casting.

The **sidearm cast** is a variation of the basic four-part or roll-cast done by holding the rod to your side so that the line travels lower and the loop lies on its side. This allows you to keep the line low and out of the fish's sight, to keep it under the wind, or to cast under obstacles.

The **backhand cast** is simply an opposite sidearm cast. The rod and casting arm are placed across your body so that the line and fly are cast to that side. This gives you the advantage of the sidearm cast with another cast angle.

The **underhand cast** is basically a sidearm cast done with an underhand casting stroke so that the line and fly travel very low or skip over the water. This is an excellent way to present a fly very delicately.

The **skip cast** is simply a sidearm cast delivered with extra-fast speed and a low angle so that the fly hits the water and skips to the target. This is a great technique for casting a fly far back under low overhanging obstructions.

A **curve cast** bends to the right or left of you and is a variation of the standard forward cast. A portion of the line tip, leader, and fly curves to the right or left from the general direction of the power-casting stroke. Curve casts are useful when presenting the fly around surface objects or to prevent the leader and fly line from being seen by a fish as the fly passes overhead.

The **slack-line** or **serpent-cast** is another variation on the standard forward cast, this one causing the line to fall on the water in a series of curves or S's. Such a cast allows the fly to float without dragging and is especially useful when casting across current or directly downstream.

The **reach-cast** presents the fly to the target area and places a portion of the leader and fly line above or below the fly's position. It is especially useful when presenting a fly across a stream that has several current speeds. Reach-casting prevents the fly from dragging downstream faster than the water on which it lands. The reach-cast is also considered a mend *during* the casting stroke—an in-air mend.

COMMON FLY-CASTING PROBLEMS AND SOLUTIONS

Proper fly-casting technique takes patience and practice to acquire. You will probably encounter difficulties along the way to achieving proficiency. Here are some of the most common problems that beginner and intermediate casters encounter. Each is followed by its solution.

Problem: Fly line, leader, and fly will not go out the desired distance (20 to 60 feet).

Solution: This is often the beginner's first problem, and it usually is caused by inefficient casting technique or improperly balanced tackle or both.

Make sure the rod and fly-line sizes are properly matched. Too light a line for a rod will cause casting problems of this nature. Check your four basic cast moves. Work on tighter loop control and better timing of power application on both the up-and-back and down-and-forward casting strokes. Also make sure you are using the correct casting plane for the distance that you are casting and for your height above the water.

Problem: Fly hits the water behind the caster.

Solution: This problem usually results from inefficiency in the up-and-back. Check to see that you are starting your pickup at eight o'clock and lifting the fly line off the water as your rod tip reaches the ten o'clock position. You want a smooth, slack-free line pickup at the beginning of the up-and-back stroke, and a quick stop of the power stroke at the twelve o'clock position. *Check how far behind you the rod tip is going.* You may be waiting too long on the up-and-back cast to allow the line to straighten. Look back to see if your backcast falls or if it has enough power to unroll before it begins to fall behind you. Remember: It takes more power to cast up-and-back than down-and-forward.

Wide up-and-back cast loop, and wide forward-and-down cast loop. Both these loops cause problems with distance and accuracy.

Problem: Leader and line splash down too hard or before they completely unroll and straighten out.

Solution: This usually indicates that you are bringing the rod tip too low during your forward stroke, thus forcing line and leader to the water before the loop unrolls. Stop the power stroke higher and delay the rod's follow-through to the eight o'clock position until the fly lands on the water.

Problem: Fly, leader, and line strike the rod.

Solution: If the line or leader strikes the rod on the backward or forward cast, first angle the fly rod to the side to avoid most line-rod collisions. You may need more power or a smoother power stroke. When lifting line from the water, be sure to begin the pickup at the eight o'clock position, then lift the line by raising the rod butt and your arm before you begin the up-and-back stroke. Now simply apply more power to the power stroke when making the up-and-back or down-and-forward casts.

Problem: Tailing loop, in which the fly, leader, and line tangle together at the end of the casting stroke.

Tailing loop. This casting fault causes most wind knot- sand line/leader/fly tangles.

Solution: This problem usually results when an inexperienced fly caster begins a power stroke before the backcast loop unrolls. With more advanced casters, the problem is most commonly a result of applying power to the rod too quickly rather than allowing the power to increase smoothly through the stroke. This is especially common when you try to cast extra distance or into a strong wind.

Watch your loop unroll, start the power stroke slowly, and gradually accelerate just as the line tip and leader are unrolling. Beginning a stroke too fast will shock the rod's tip and cause it to recoil, which drops that point of the fly line and forms a tailing loop.

Problem: Too wide a loop.

Solution: This problem results from a power-stroke arc that is too wide. The loop size is proportional to the size of the rod-tip arc. Using the clock method, practice the power-stroke arc between the ten o'clock and twelve o'clock positions.

Problem: Leader does not straighten and piles up on the water.

Fly-line loop unrolling forward too high above water caused by high stroking when up-and-back cast has been angled too low. Line, leader, and fly usually fall short of target and land in a pile.

Solution: This is usually caused by either too wide a loop or your down-and-forward power-stroke direction being angled too high above the water. Try to apply power more down and toward the target, and tighten your loop.

Problem: Open loop.

Solution: This problem is caused by too wide a rod-tip arc when casting, or by starting the casting stroke too late, then exaggerating by lowering your tip too quickly after the power stroke. It may be solved in the same manner as the problem of casting too wide a loop. Also, make sure to leave the rod tip high (ten o'clock) until the fly and leader land on the water, so as not to pull the loop open.

Open loop. Loop has a wide, almost double-size loop shape because the fly-rod tip is far too low. As a result, the presentation is sloppy.

Wide-looped up-and-back cast. This is caused because the rod angle is almost to 3 o'clock. Watching the cast will help correct this fault.

Problem: Fly snaps off on your down-and-forward cast, and/or you hear a cracking noise on your backcast.

Solution: This happens when you start the down-and-forward cast too soon, before the line has unrolled and straightened behind you. This problem is very similar to the tailing-loop problem and can be corrected in the same manner. Get into the habit of watching your backcast, especially if you are encountering persistent casting problems. You will notice that the fly-snapping problem and line-cracking problem do not occur on the forward loop, because you watch it unroll before beginning the next stroke.

Problem: Fly and leader twist and tangle.

Solution: This happens when you use a fly that spins as it is cast. Use a fly that is designed better, or use a larger-diameter, stiffer tippet. If you can't do either, make slower casts and reduce or eliminate false-casting. Large-hackle (size 12 or larger) dry flies and flies with long upright wings or split wings are usually the worst for twisting.

Wind Casting

Excessive wind from any direction may cause casting difficulties. In most instances, however, if you understand how wind affects casting, you can use the wind to your advantage.

Problem: When the wind is in your face, it blows the fly and line back at you when you cast forward.

Solution: To avoid this, increase the height and angle of the up-and-back cast. This tactic lofts the line into the wind, adding its force to the backcast, which enhances the forward-cast power. Make the down-and-forward cast more directly toward the water. Always form a tight loop when casting into the wind.

Problem: When the wind is at your back, it tends to slow and blow the fly line down, causing it to strike your back or the rod on a forward stroke.

Solution: Make a powerful sidearm, low-angle, tight-loop up-and-back stroke to reduce wind drag on the line and to keep the line out of the wind's full force— just the opposite of casting into the wind. On the forward-and-down stroke make a higher-angle power stroke to let the wind's force lift and turn over the line, leader, and fly. If the wind is too strong for a good cast, simply make a forward roll-cast to let the fly line roll and blow forward with the wind.

Problem: When the wind is from your casting-arm side, it blows the line across your body and head, often tangling up or hooking you.

Solution: To correct this, keep the rod and arm high and angled over you to the other side or use a backhand casting technique. You can also use the opposite arm for casting. These adaptations place the line on the downwind side of you and prevent it from striking you.

Problem: When the wind blows from your free-arm side, the line is blown low and to the rod's side, causing a presentation problem or the possibility of hooking someone on that side.

Solution: To solve this problem, use a low sidearm cast to reduce the fly-line height, which avoids the wind's full force. The fly line is blown out farther to that side, so you only need to compensate for extra wind lead.

The wind's force against any cast is best countered using a very tight-looped and powerful (high line speed) cast. The modern graphite fly rod is a powerful, small-diameter, high-energy casting tool and thus is the best choice during windy conditions. If you regularly fly fish in very windy areas, you should also consider using heavier line weights and faster-action rods to gain more casting power against the wind. It is very hard to make long and accurate casts against strong wind (20 miles per hour or more). But if you follow these suggestions, there is no reason that you cannot enjoy fly casting in normal winds of 5 to 10 miles per hour.

4
FLY-FISHING TACTICS

Fishing the fly is as important as casting the fly. Unless you intend to fly cast only in your backyard or to be a tournament fly caster, you will need to become a student of the ways of water and of fish and fish foods.

▼

There are two types of fly-fishing water: still water and moving water. Lakes, streams, and oceans have both types. Still water is less common than moving water, even in a lake, because of wind and currents. Oceans have currents, tides, and inflows.

Presenting a fly in calm water involves casting to a certain spot and then allowing the fly to rest, or swimming it back toward you. In still water, your fly, leader, and line remain motionless until you move them. The successful fly fisher works the fly at the right depth and with an action that imitates what the fish are feeding on. Drag is seldom a problem on still water unless the wind is blowing or you are moving, as in a drifting boat. Then you must adjust your retrieving technique as if you were fishing on flowing water.

Achieving good results in moving water requires many casting and presentation techniques. In such water, at or below the surface, the fly is fished by letting it simply move with the current's direction and speed, or is retrieved across, down, or directly against the current.

The natural movements of fish foods range from stationary to swimming up, down, or across currents. Imitating such actions with fly tackle is simple. At certain times and places, fish will respond aggressively to a fly fished with an unnatural action, but these instances are both less predictable and less common than are reactions to true imitations of natural fish food.

The fly fisher who prefers to fish moving water should be familiar with three basic fly presentations.

Practicing with water targets greatly speeds up learning the accurate presentations required to catch fish consistently.

The **upstream presentation** is one in which the fly is cast upstream to or above the area in which you suspect a fish is waiting. Generally, the upstream presentation allows the fly to float or drift downstream at the speed, and under the control, of the water's flow.

The **downstream presentation** is one in which the fly is cast downstream just above or to the area that you suspect holds a fish. With this presentation, the fly can be retrieved upstream, retrieved to the right or left across the stream, or, by paying out fly line, allowed to drift downstream.

The **across-stream presentation** is one in which the fly is cast at an angle across the current to land just above where you suspect a fish is waiting. Variations of the across-stream presentation allow the fly to drift downstream, be retrieved upstream, or be retrieved across stream.

APPROACHING YOUR QUARRY

Fly fishers must approach their quarry more closely and quietly than other anglers do, for successful presentation of the fly. Most fly fishing is done either

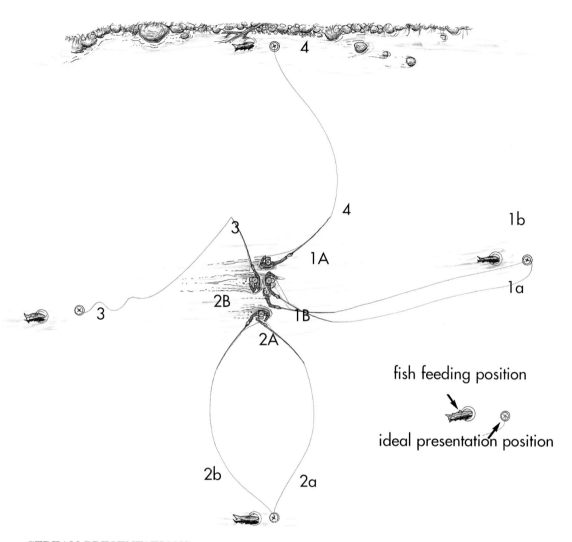

fish feeding position

ideal presentation position

STREAM PRESENTATIONS

1. **Upstream to fish:** *1A. (the cast) 1a. (the presentation) Standing directly below the fish's position, make a curve cast. 1B. (the cast) 1b. (the presentation) Standing several feet to the right or left of the fish's position, make a straight cast.*

2. **Across-stream, right:** *2A. (the cast) 2a. (the presentation) Use an upstream reach cast when the fish is in a slower current than the fly line. 2B. (the cast) 2b. (the presentation) Use a downstream reach cast when the fish is in faster water than the fly line. Mending is recommended in both cases.*

3. **Downstream:** *Use a slack line cast, short of the fish, then lower your rod as the fly floats toward the fish. (Do not stand directly above the fish if possible.)*

4. **Across-stream, left:** *Casting toward the shoreline, use an upstream reach cast if the fish is in slower water than the fly line. Mending is also recommended to continue a long, drag-free drift.*

by walking along shorelines or by wading, and generally these approaches are the least complicated and most satisfying. However, some waters are too deep or distant to approach on foot. For these places the fly fisher must use a flotation device. Here are a few of the best alternative approach methods.

Float tubes are the most popular and economical means of safe and convenient personal floatation.

Float tubes are round or U-shaped one-person, portable, and inflatable flotation units in which the angler sits. They are propelled with swim fins or ankle paddles. Float tubes are excellent for approaching fish closely and quietly on sheltered, still water, but are not recommended or safe for flowing water. They are lightweight and economical and are also a good choice for ponds and lakes where it is difficult or impossible to launch other types of boats.

Kick boats are portable and inflatable one-person crafts that the angler sits *on* and propels with either swim fins or oars or both. Kick boats are larger and more buoyant than float tubes, so the angler sits higher above the water, with only the legs below the knees in the water; this usually makes it easier to cast and warmer when the water is cold. Kick boats can also move faster across the water. Most are for still water, but some can be used in rivers if you are a skilled boater and cautious about attempting swift and treacherous rapids. Another convenience is that there is room to carry extra equipment, often even a cooler.

A distinct advantage to using a float tube or kick boat is that everyone gets to fish because no one has to "row the boat." Of course it's not possible, convenient, or desirable to use float tubes and kick boats in some fishing situations. The following devices require a rower.

Inflatable rafts are larger than kick boats and are designed to float or drift streams; they usually carry more than one person. They are powered by oars and/or small outboard engines. Rafts are a convenient method for fly fishing while drifting down a river or for getting to hard-to-reach wade-fishing areas.

Prams are small one- or two-person cartop boats that are propelled by oars or a small outboard motor. They are useful in sheltered still water and slow-flowing streams, or to reach wadeable water.

A kick boat.

Canoes are one- and two-person lightweight, cartop crafts that are traditional classics for fly fishing ponds, lakes, streams, and rivers. Canoes are easily paddled and can be adapted for small outboard motors to cover longer expanses of water. They are quiet, graceful, and beautiful boats to enjoy fly fishing from or to use to reach distant wading waters.

Johnboats are flat-bottomed wooden or aluminum boats with squared bow and stern and can usually accommodate two to four persons. They are powered by pole, paddle, electric motor, or gas engine. The flat bottom of a johnboat makes it ideally stable for reaching shallow waters and fly fishing; but it is not comfortable to use on high waves.

Canoes are the ideal shallow draft boats for one or two anglers to access good fly-fishing areas of lakes and streams with speed and quietness.

McKenzie River drift boats are rowboats that are specifically designed for floating or drifting streams and rivers. They are ideal for one or two fly fishers and an oarsman. They are flat bottomed and shallow drafted, and they offer precise maneuverability with oars. Many are fitted with specific devices for fly-fishing comfort—such as swivel seats and slots for standing anglers.

A johnboat.

McKenzie drift boats are very stable crafts to drift streams with. You can cast from them or beach them and wade.

A bass boat.

Bass boats are large, shallow-drafted, stable fiberglass or aluminum boats with casting decks on the bow and stern. They are powered by large gas engines and electric fishing motors. They are good crafts for larger lakes, especially when fly fishers must travel some distance to reach the waters they wish to fish.

Flats skiffs are similar to bass boats except with even shallower drafts and cleaner interiors—and they are a bit more seaworthy for fishing saltwater bays, flats, and brackish backwaters. For fly fishing, skiffs are usually poled, but some are also powered by electric fishing motors.

TECHNIQUES FOR FISHING FLIES

Artificial flies can deceive fish into mistaking them for the real thing. There are five basic kinds of flies: dry flies, wet flies, nymphs, streamers, and bugs.

Dry flies float on or in the surface to imitate terrestrial or aquatic insects. Generally, such insects float and move with the water's surface movements or with the wind's speed and direction. Dry flies are usually presented with a floating fly line and allowed to drift or float as naturally as possible. If the real insect is active on the surface, you should attempt to impart a similar action to the artificial. On the other hand, if the natural is inactive, the imitation should also be inactive. Wind, variable horizontal current speeds, or both of these forces will often cause drag on the fly line, leader, and fly. Drag causes the imitation to move unnaturally. It can usually be avoided by proper presentation and mending of the fly line.

Most dry flies are designed and tied with materials that allow them to float partly above or in the water's surface film. However, if not treated with a

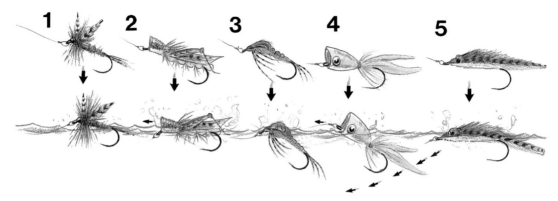

Examples of how **floating-fly designs** rest on or in the water's surface.

1. Hackled Dry Fly: sits on the surface
2. Grasshopper: swims in surface
3. Emergent Nymph: hangs in surface film
4. Bass Popper: pops and swims across surface
5. Frog Diver: floats on and dives below surface.

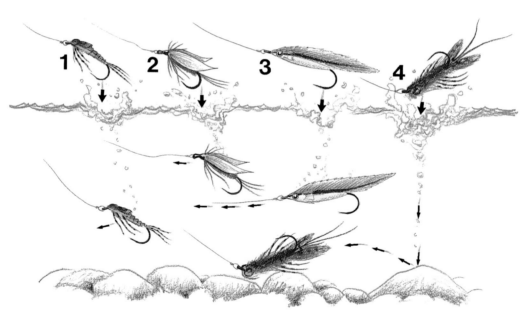

How **sinking flies** sink and swim below the water surface.

1. Weighted Nymph: sinks and swims or drifts
2. Wet Fly: sinks slowly and swims or drifts
3. Streamer: sinks and swims like a small fish
4. Fast Sinking Crayfish: sinks to the bottom and crawls or swims near bottom.

waterproofing agent such as silicone or paraffin, they usually will soon become wet and sink. This is especially true when a fly has undergone repeated dunkings or has caught many fish. Use a dry-fly spray or paste to waterproof the fly before you use it. Put on just enough to coat the entire fly very lightly. Sprays and liquids are a little easier to apply, but they are more expensive and do not last as long as the paste dry-fly flotants. Pastes will usually liquefy with the warmth of your fingers and solidify when fished.

If the dry fly begins to float too low or sink and does not improve after several water-removing false-casts, retrieve it and blot with an absorbent paper or cloth towel, tissue, or chamois leather. Absorbing the excess water will lighten the fly and serve also to clean it. Apply another coat of dry-fly dressing, and the fly should float like new. An absorbent towel or chamois is also very useful for cleaning and drying the fly after you remove it—wet, slimy, and matted—from a fish's mouth.

Wet flies sink just below the surface or deeper and generally imitate aquatic insects swimming, emerging, egg-laying, or drifting helplessly in the water. Some wet flies also imitate small fish or submerged terrestrial insects. Wet flies can be fished with floating, sinking-tip, or full-sinking fly lines, depending upon the depth and angle of the desired fly movement. On calm water, wet flies are usually presented *on the far side* of where you suspect a fish is swimming. The fly is then allowed to sink to the right depth. Then, with whatever action and speed will imitate the natural insect or small minnow, the fly is retrieved to and past the fish. Many wet flies are made in highly colorful attractor or exciter patterns, especially those used for brook trout, bass, shad, panfish, salmon, and steelhead. These attractor flies are generally fished faster and in a less imitative manner in an attempt to attract and excite the fish.

Wet flies in moving water are generally presented *in front of and just above* the fish's position. They are drifted downstream or retrieved across or upstream, depending upon what they are designed to imitate and how they are meant to attract or excite the fish. Some wet-fly methods use more than one fly on the leader. (Check regulations for waters you fish.) Sometimes as many as six wet flies are used, although two flies are much more common. Multiple wet flies are usually fished on and just below the surface.

Nymphs are designed to be fished below the surface, including on the bottom, of either calm or moving water. Nymphs mainly suggest (give a general impression) or imitate (give a detailed impression) immature aquatic insects. But nymphs also may be used to suggest snails, scuds, leeches, crayfish, worms, and similar foods. Floating, intermediate, sinking-tip, and full-sinking fly lines are useful in various waters to fish nymphs. For shallow, still, and moving water from 1 to 6 feet deep, the floating or intermediate lines are generally best. These lines allow the best overall fly action and control for nymphing. For medium depth (4 to 8 feet), especially in moving water, the sinking-tip fly line generally works best. For deeper water (8 to 20 feet), either still or moving, a full-sinking line generally performs best with nymphs.

In still water, the nymph is cast *past* the fish's swimming path or holding area. It is allowed to sink to the desired depth, then it is animated with the method that best suggests the live natural food.

In moving water, nymphs are fished in two basic ways. In the first method they are fished with a floating line. The nymph is cast *upstream* and allowed to sink and drift naturally downstream. The second way is with a sinking-tip or full-sinking line. The nymph is cast up and across stream to achieve the tight line-to-leader-to-fly contact needed to animate a nymph with a swimming action while retrieving it across or upstream.

Streamers are usually designed to be fished below the surface to suggest or imitate the small fish, minnows, eels, leeches, and so on, that are swimming or drifting in the water. However, streamers are sometimes fished at the surface to imitate the feeding or crippled action of a small fish. Streamers, like nymphs, can be fished with all four fly-line types depending upon the action and the depth desired. The sinking tip is generally the best all-around streamer fly line.

In still water the streamer is presented *near or beyond* the fish's position and is retrieved *past and away from* the fish with an action that suggests the natural creature's panic or vulnerability.

In moving water the streamer may be presented at all angles to suggest the natural food's movement. Most small fish are strong swimmers and can live in areas from top to bottom in a stream. Perhaps the most popular streamer presentation is casting across the current and retrieving with erratic swimming and pausing action as the fly swims and swings down and across the flow. This sideways motion suggests distress and vulnerability to a minnow-hungry fish. Once the streamer reaches the end of the drift, it is retrieved erratically upstream. Sometimes streamers are effective when cast upstream and allowed to drift downstream with the current , as if they were dying or helpless.

Wet flies, nymphs, and streamers perform best when they are tied using soft, water-absorbent materials. After they get wet, they take on the natural odors of the waters you fish. Before you begin fishing these three types, rub them on a wet algae-covered stone, on some aquatic vegetation, or on some silt taken from the bottom of the water you plan to fish. This simple wetting and deodorizing preparation will enhance your fly's ability to fool fish.

Bugs float on the surface and suggest larger insects, frogs, mice, crippled minnows, and so on. Bugs are fished with a floating or sinking-tip fly line. Use a floating line if you're fishing bugs just at the surface. A sinking-tip fly line, with a 4- to 6-foot leader, allows the fly to be fished at the surface, diving, swimming, or surfacing.

For stillwater fishing, bugs are generally presented *near or past* the fish's location. Often they are most effective when presented near structures such as the bank, lily pads, logs, or overhanging trees. When cast over an object, a bug can be hopped or made to fall into the water to suggest a natural terrestrial food falling into the water. Once on the surface, the bug is worked like a miniature puppet, being made to struggle or swim in an attempt to entice a strike. Usually, the more slowly these types of flies are moved, the more effective they are.

In moving water, bugs are generally cast at all current and eddy angles and fished with an action similar to what is used in still water. Line drag is avoided by casting-angle adjustments and line mending, as with dry flies. In moving water, bugs are usually fished near or off shoreline and surface structures.

Dropper flies (two or more flies) may be used on one leader to increase your chances of catching one or more fish on a cast. (Check regulations first.) Such combinations as two to four wet flies, wet fly and streamer, nymph and streamer, or dry fly and nymph are often more effective than a single fly. The larger, heavier fly should always be tied to the end of the leader and the smaller, lighter flies tied farther up the leader's tippet (except in the case of a dropper tied to the hook or eye of another fly). A dropper fly is attached to a leader by first tying a blood knot or surgeon's knot with a 4- to 6-inch tag of tippet material. The fly is then tied onto the long tag with a Duncan loop or improved clinch knot (see chapter 2, page 40).

By using two or three flies at one time on your leader's tip and tippet, you can learn what the fish's preference is from repeated catches on one of the flies. Many times two, three, or four flies will also have an "emotional" or exciting effect on fish that might ignore a single fly. Casting two or more flies is, however, a bit more difficult than casting one fly and tangles are more frequent.

ANIMATING FLIES, DETECTING STRIKES, AND HOOKING AND FIGHTING FISH

Once you have learned to cast a fly correctly and accurately and can quickly establish the two-point control, your focus shifts to making the fly look desirable to the fish, detecting the strike, hooking the fish, tiring it, then landing it.

Fly animation is normally accomplished in either a passive or an active manner. The **passive** method involves simply letting the fly sit or drift with current or wind, allowing the fly to float or sink and move in the water more or less as would a helpless insect or injured live food.

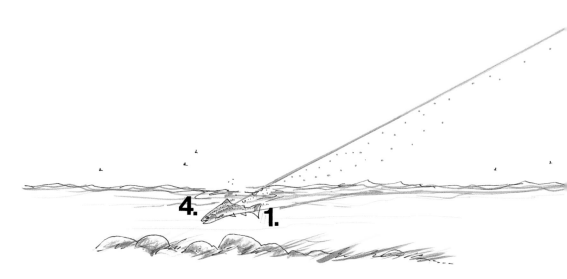

Small-hook strike and set procedure

1. *Angler detects fish strike by feeling it on line or by seeing it.*
2. *Rod tip position as strike occurs may be between 8:00 and 10:00 depending on the type of water and fish.*
3. *Strike with rod by quickly and crisply lifting and rotating the rod tip upward to 11:00. The high tip position absorbs some of the excess energy to prevent break-offs.*
3a. *As the rod is lifted up and the tip rotated, allow a few inches of slack fly line to slip from your line hand. This helps prevent the tippet from snapping and keeps the hook from bending or being pulled out of the fish.*
4. *Fish is hooked and begins to tire quickly against the spring of the high rod.*

The **active** method involves puppeteering the fly, either by pulling on the fly line with your line hand or by careful rod-tip movements. Perfecting these fly-animation techniques is fascinating and challenging, second only to casting for pure enjoyment. Seeing a fish leap to meet your fly as it falls to the water, intercept its drift, or chase and catch it is always thrilling.

Detecting these "bites" is the key to hooking fish. The first sense to use is your sight. Watch your fly if you can see it; if not, watch your leader, strike indicator, or fly line for any unnatural movement that might indicate a fish has taken the fly. Next, feel and listen for strikes. The line and rod provide you with a sensitive connection to the fly. Strikes may be no more than a slight tightening or

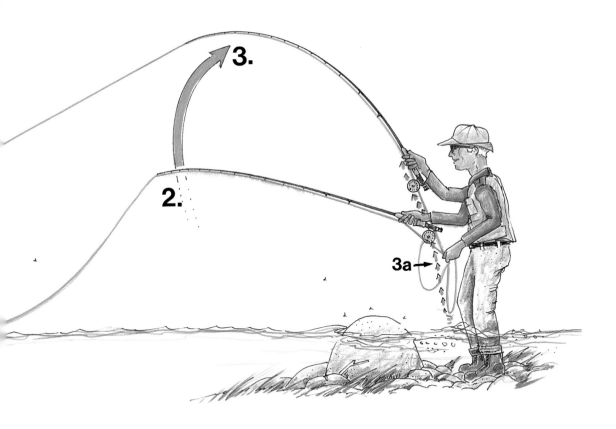

loosening of line tension—a twitch or a series of tugs. You must recognize these and react *immediately* with a strike. If you delay even a second, the fish will usually recognize a fake and spit it out.

The major mistake fly-fishing students make is in not concentrating on and reacting to these takes. At my schools I have students practice recognizing strikes by sight, feel, and sound, reacting quickly and reflexively.

Setting the Hook

When a fish takes a fly, you seldom have more than two or three seconds to hook it before it ejects the fake food. You must react quickly to make the point of the hook penetrate the fish's mouth. We call this **setting the hook.** Smaller and barbless hooks require less energy to hook most fish. Larger hooks require more energy or power even for the smaller fish.

Small flies (sizes 18 to 8) usually require finer leader tips to be most effective. Smaller hooks also require *less* energy to penetrate a fish's mouth skin. The light-leader, small-hook strike is a *quick* movement up and back with the fly-rod tip—not a slow pull. This up-and-back movement hooks the fish and puts the rod in a position to absorb any excess pulls from you or the fish that might break the leader or tear the fly out of the fish's mouth.

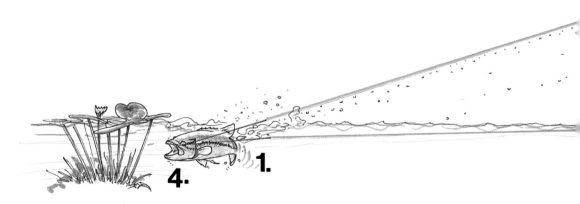

Large-hook strike and set procedure

1. *Angler detects strike by feeling or seeing it.*
2. *As strike is detected, immediately pull line taut with line hand. Note that the rod tip is low and that the line is tight to the fish.*
3. *With stern force on the rod's mid and butt, pull it back and up (to your side and back) to position 3 of the diagram (around 10 or 10:30).*
4. *Fish is hooked and rod is in ideal position to assert more hooking force or leverage against the fish in order to tire it quickly.*

Large flies (sizes 6 to 5/0) usually require much more strike energy to penetrate the fish's mouth tissue, and also a different strike method than small hooks. The large fly hook is set with a quick line-hand pull on the fly line followed immediately by a stern back motion of the rod's mid- and butt sections while keeping the tip low and forward. This strike motion and low tip angle put much more force on the hook's point, causing the hook to move forward and penetrate a fish's mouth.

In both cases the hook penetrates faster if the strike begins with a quick move. Think of the difference between driving a nail into wood by striking it sharply with a hammer or just pushing on it.

When you see, feel, or even sense the fish take your fly, you must be prepared to set the hook *quickly!* Lack of concentration often prevents strike detection and quick reaction. It is important to practice striking and setting the hook until it becomes a *reflex action*. A pond full of small panfish such as bluegill or sunfish is ideal for this practice.

Remember, striking and setting the hook on most fish requires a quick tightening of the fly line with the rod and line hand. Larger or tough-mouthed fish

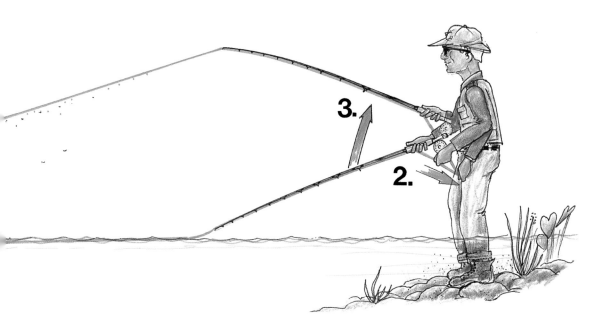

require a stronger, harder rod strike performed while also pulling down on the fly line with your free hand. Very sharp barbless hooks are vastly more efficient in hooking fish than are dull or barbed hooks. For the same reason—less friction in penetrating the fish's mouth tissue—smaller hooks require less force to set than do larger hooks regardless of the fish's size. Overreacting when striking a large fish with a small line and a light leader will usually result in breaking the leader and losing the fish.

Landing Fish

Once the fish is securely hooked, it will struggle to escape. Landing small fish is rarely a problem. But larger fish have the size and strength to take out line, dive under cover, or break your leader. Your skill counters these maneuvers. This is one of the most pleasurable and exciting parts of angling.

Always maintain a taut line on the fish in order to keep the hook embedded and the fish under your control. Know the power of your rod and strength of your leader tip. Do not exceed these limits when fighting a large fish. Try to keep the rod at about a 45-degree angle above the water so the rod tip can absorb the tension of the fighting fish on the hook and leader. If the fish pulls harder than your tackle can stand, let it pull out line until it tires, slows, or stops. Then immediately resume pulling it in.

Never force in a fish, but rather allow it to jump, swim, and struggle until tired. Don't try to boss a freshly hooked fish or it is likely to panic and break away. Likewise, never underplay the fish. Use enough rod and line pressure to make the fish struggle and tire quickly. When fighting a fish in a stream or river, try to position yourself to its side or below it. Fighting a fish upstream will take longer and could give the fish the advantage it needs to get off the hook. It can also cause the fish to become overtired and drown.

It is a good practice, after you get a fish under control, to fight it directly from the fly reel, rather than to strip in slack line that might tangle around your feet or legs. This is especially true for larger fish. Do not just reel the fish straight in. Instead, pump the fish in with the rod, first lifting it up then reeling in line as you let the rod down.

When the hooked fish tires, it will begin swimming slightly on its side. *Do not reel the fish all the way to the rod tip.* Leave the leader outside the rod's tip-top, and leave at least a rod length of line and leader between you and the fish. That way the line and leader should have enough stretch to keep from breaking, and the knots will not hang in the guides if the fish makes an unexpected dash. This length also allows you to reach the fish as you land it.

When the fish is ready to be landed, it will reluctantly but calmly surface and lack the strength to dive away. Depending on its species, size, and location, several methods can be used.

Catch and Release

For various personal, sporting, or legal reasons, you may wish to release a fish. It is important for you to know how. To release a small fish, if the hook is visible in the fish's mouth, pull the fish close to you in the water. Then simply reach out, grasp the fly, and turn and twist the hook upward. The hook will disengage (this is especially easy if the hook is barbless) and the fish will turn head-down and swim away. If the hook is deeper, secure the fish by gently sliding your wet hand under its stomach and lifting without squeezing its body. Avoid putting your fingers inside the fish's mouth or through its gills to free the hook, and try not to lift the fish out of the water. Most fish, even small trout, have sharp teeth or gill rakers that can cause painful or even crippling cuts. Besides, fish are very likely to thrash when they feel your hands. This action can result in your hooking yourself or dropping the fish and injuring it. Use a hook-removal tool instead. With a hook disgorger or a hemostat, firmly grasp the fly and back the hook out. Quickly place the fish back in the water and give it time to regain its equilibrium and swim out of your hand.

When releasing a fish, never *throw* it back into the water. The fish is tired from the fight, and the shock of hitting the water lessens its chances of survival. A small landing net is very useful for landing and releasing small fish. To release a large fish (16 inches or more), use a specially designed catch-and-release landing net, with a soft, shallow bag, or carefully beach the fish if you don't have a net.

The catch-and-release net is an ideal tool to land, unhook, and release a trout.

Netting: Lead the tired fish with steady, smooth rod pressure over the bag of a still, submerged net. As the fish's head comes over the net's bag, release the rod tension so that the fish's head will begin to sink into the net. At the same time, lift up the net to trap the entire body. Never come down on or from behind a fish with the net; this kind of approach can strike and frighten the fish and cause it to swim or leap away from the net. Keep most of the net's bag in the water until the fish calms down. Reach inside and unhook the fish, trying to keep the fish's body and gills in the water.

Let the fish revive and swim out of the net bag under its own power; dumping or tossing a fish out of a net can injure it.

Beaching: When the fish surfaces and turns on its side, calmly and gently lead it with steady rod pressure to a gradually sloping, unobstructed shoreline. As the fish beaches itself in the shallows, relax the line pull. Unhook the fish and turn it around, gently coaxing it into deeper water. If the fish is too exhausted to right itself and swim, hold it upright (with your hand near the tail) until it does. Then let it escape your gentle hold under its own power.

Never pull a fish you intend to release completely out of the water onto the shore. If you must handle it, do so as tenderly as you would a human infant. Never hold a fish by sticking your fingers inside the gills. Try not to keep an exhausted fish out of the water any longer than you absolutely must. If you wish to show your catch to a companion or photograph it, keep the fish in the water until you actually show it or photograph it. I recommend that you prefocus and set the aperture before you photograph the fish; this can save precious time out of the water.

If the fish is hooked in the gills or throat, to ensure that it has the best chance to survive you should cut the leader at the hook eye, then release the fish. In time the fish's immune system and enzymes will reject the hook and the wound will heal. If hooking or hook removal causes continuous bleeding, the fish most likely will die.

Catch and Keep

If you plan to keep a fish, you should tire it thoroughly before attempting to land it. It is best to use a landing net on freshwater fish such as trout, bass, walleye, pike, and panfish. Most smaller saltwater fish can also be landed with a net.

Once the fish is in the net and calms down, you can remove the fly hook using the procedure already described for releasing a fish. If the fish is not put in a live well or on a stringer, it is best to kill it immediately. Do this by striking it several times on the top of its head, just behind the eyes, with a small club, or priest.

To beach a fish that you wish to keep, *thoroughly tire it out.* Follow the procedure described earlier for catch-and-release beaching, except use more force and beach the fish farther up on the shore. Extra tiring will prevent the fish from flopping back in. A sharp rap on the head will stun or kill a beached fish.

Many larger freshwater and saltwater fish that you wish to land and keep require the use of either a tailer or a gaff. A **tailer** is a device that is commonly used by Atlantic salmon anglers to disable and hold the salmon with its tail in a loop snare. A **gaff** is a large metal hook with a sturdy handle for hooking (gaffing) and landing a large fish. The gaff is a more brutal way to land a fish, especially if used to hook the fish's body, but it is sometimes necessary on strong, large, and dangerous fish such as shark, billfish, and tuna. Gaffs can be used to lip-hook larger fish without seriously wounding them if they are to be photographed and/or released. It is more difficult to use a gaff or tailer than to use a net or the beaching method. We do not advise using gaff or tailer without personal instruction from an experienced fly fisher or fishing guide.

The **priest**—actually a fancy club—is used to kill or stun a large fish immediately after it is tailed or gaffed. Strike the fish on the head just between and behind the eyes. Failure to

TIPS ON TERMINAL FLY TACKLE

One of the most frequent mistakes new fly fishers make is not regularly checking their tackle for possible problems. Here are some things to look for.

- Check the fly regularly, especially if it is not drawing strikes or you are missing strikes. Check for a broken hook, dull or bent hook point, moss or weeds on the fly, a tangle with the leader, or fly parts wrapped around the hook bend. Also look for any damage that might affect the fly's looks or action.

- Check your knots, particularly your fly-to-tippet and tippet-to-tip knots, after landing several small or large fish or after extended casting periods. Knots weaken or slip when wet, from overtightening, and from abrasion.

- Check your leader for cuts, abrasions, or wind knots.

use a priest can result in personal injury or equipment damage from a large fish thrashing about out of the water.

COMMON FLY-FISHING PROBLEMS AND SOLUTIONS

Problem: Scaring fish.

Solution: This is a problem most fly fishers encounter until they recognize that fish are frightened by their presence and noise as well as by the disturbance made in fly casting and presentation.

Stay low, move slowly and quietly, and wear clothes that do not contrast with the background. Try to cast so that your rod and line are not easily visible to the fish. Make your presentation softly, and keep your fly line and leader from splashing or floating over a fish.

Problem: Missing strikes.

Solution: Keep your fly hooks extremely sharp and stay *constantly alert*. Be ready the instant a fish takes the fly. Avoid excessive slack line. Practice striking quickly. Also regularly check to see if your hook point is dulled or broken from striking stones on your backcast. Polarized sunglasses are a great aid in seeing strikes and fish. Most students miss strikes simply because they do not react promptly and set the hook when they see or feel the fish seize the fly.

Problem: Breaking off fish on the strike.

Solution: Use less force when you strike, and make sure your hooks are very sharp. Do not strike harder on a large fish than is needed to set the hook on a similar but smaller fish. It's human nature to overreact to the sight of a big fish with a big strike. Try to stay calm. If breakoffs persist, you might increase the strength of your leader tippet. Tie your knots very carefully, and test them before fishing the fly. Check your tippet for wind knots regularly. Wind knots can weaken your leader by 50 percent.

Replace the tippet if it has a wind knot or an abrasion. Failure to do so will surely cause loss of fly or fly and fish.

- Check the leader for twists or curls, and straighten them by stroking the leader tight with your fingers and palm. Twists or curls cause the fly to cast poorly and land off-target. If these will not straighten, replace them with a new leader or tippet.

- Check for fly-line tangles on or around the fly reel as well as around the rod between the guides.

- At least twice a day, check to see if the rod's ferrules are tight, if the guides are lined up, and if the reel is still tight on the handle.

- Look behind you! This is necessary to avoid poor up-and-back casts, hanging your fly in trees, or hooking people or animals that stand or walk behind you.

Also, a longer tippet will have more "give," and will absorb mistakes better than a short one. Some fly fishers now put about 6 inches of Shockgum into the butt of their leader to prevent such breakoffs.

Problem: Hooks breaking.

Solution: This is a common problem for beginners and experts alike. It occurs when the fly is allowed to drop and strike stones on the backcast.

    Keep your up-and-back power stroke higher, and use a bit more power to keep the cast up. Sometimes the hooks will break on hooked fish; this happens because of poor hook quality or, more likely, because of improper placement and excessive tightening in a fly-tying vise when it was made.

Problem: Dry flies float poorly or sink.

Solution: If dry flies are properly constructed and waterproofed, they should float well. You may be presenting the fly too forcefully and thus dunking it on impact. Make sure the fly is well waterproofed with dry-fly spray or paste. Present the fly about 2 feet above the water so it will alight softly. When you pick it up, make one or two quick, brisk false-casts to shake the water out of it. This tactic does not necessarily dry it completely but reduces its weight so it will alight softly again on the next presentation. After you catch a fish on the fly, blot off the slime and water with a soft paper towel, a chamois, or a tissue before casting it again. Check also to see if your fly-line tip may be sinking. This can cause your fly to go under, too. Add paste line flotant to the line tip to help it float.

Problem: Dry flies dragging and scaring rising fish.

Solution: When a dry fly moves across, up, or down the current unnaturally, it is *dragging* and will often scare a rising fish. Make your presentation with more slack leader, and learn to mend a surface line that is moving faster or slower than the fly to gain a natural drift speed.

Problem: Line and fly won't come off the water easily. This results from your floating line sinking. It may not be straight because of reel memory, or it may have become coated with particles of dirt.

Solution: Clean your fly line with a damp cloth or soapy rag. Wipe the line dry and apply some fly-line flotant or polish. The fly line will float higher and pick up much more easily when it's kept clean and coated with flotant. You might also practice lifting the fly line out of the water more slowly and smoothly. (For straightening instructions see chapter 2, Assembling Fly Tackle.)

Problem: Fly goes too deep and hangs up on the bottom.

Solution: In still water, do not allow the fly to sink so long. Retrieve a bit faster. In flowing water, cast the fly with a little less angle upstream or start your retrieve sooner.

Problem: Sinking fly lines and heavily weighted flies are difficult to pick up.

Solution: Pull more of the line in past your rod's tip-top and use a short roll-cast to lift the remainder. As the roll reaches the line's tip, initiate a regular pick-up to begin your backcast. This procedure will work well for any type of fly that is difficult to pick up.

READING WATER

Reading water begins with the choice of what water to fish and when. All fish are cold-blooded and must live and feed according to season, weather, water temperature, and water volume. You should learn the seasonal requirements of fish in the water you plan to visit.

Once you are on the water, there are several ways you can read it. First, you must learn to recognize the overall *structure* of any area of a lake, stream, canal, bay, or ocean. Structure is what lies along the perimeter, lies on the bottom, or extends up from or down to the bottom. Structure may be rocks, moss beds, fallen trees, or other such natural or unnatural objects. It is around these structures that fish and their foods live. Food is more plentiful here, and the structure provides protection from predators.

Eddies and pools created by structures provide relief from strong currents. Spawning often takes place in these same fertile, protected areas. To find fish, learn to recognize major structure areas. Many anglers regularly use sonar units, or fish-finders, to locate underwater structure and fish in waters too deep or murky to see well. The "sidefinder" units are most practical for fly fishing.

Clear water looks darker with an increase in depth. Water depth, bottom structures, and the fish's own color meet most of the protection and concealment needs of fish. Polarized sunglasses are a great aid to your seeing through the reflective water surface. If fish are not clearly visible at the surface or in the shallow water, they most likely will be hidden in the deeper, darker water. Since fish often have camouflage coloration, they will not be easy to see. The key to seeing fish is to watch for their movements and shadows on the bottom as much as (or more than) you watch for the actual fish.

In streams, the water's surface tells you how fast the water is moving and what structures might lie unseen in the murky or dark water. A large underwater

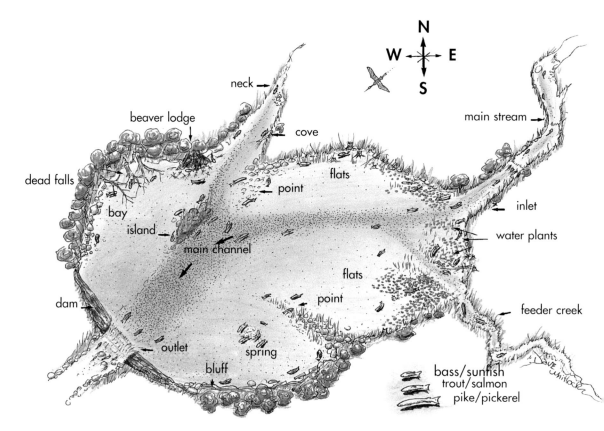

FRESHWATER LAKE
Typical structures and fish locations

boulder or log, for example, will cause surface irregularities. Flowing water usually moves fastest at the surface and slowest at the bottom. In streams, fish are usually found during feeding periods in moderate riffles, pocket waters, and runs; along the shoreline of pools; on flats; or in the pool tails. When they are resting or in nonfeeding periods, you may still entice strikes by fishing in deep pocket water, slower riffles, and runs, and down a pool's channel. Springwater inflows can attract fish in streams as it does in lakes.

Reading water, therefore, involves seeing fish or evidence of their presence, or identifying areas that are likely to hold fish. Good water reading can save hours of unproductive fishing.

In lakes, fish are usually found feeding at inlets along weedy or rocky shorelines, over and around offshore weed beds, just off points, and up in coves. If the wind is blowing, they usually feed beneath the surface on the downwind

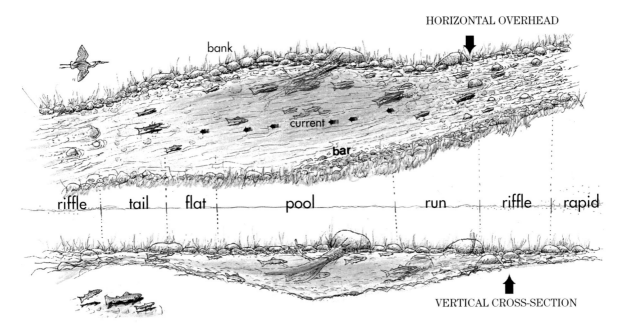

HORIZONTAL OVERHEAD

bank

current

bar

riffle | tail | flat | pool | run | riffle | rapid

VERTICAL CROSS-SECTION

These are typical freshwater stream sections with structures that are probable fish locations.

side and on the surface on the upwind side. During nonfeeding periods, you catch fish in the deeper channels by fishing your fly deep or near the bottom. Natural springs seeping up from lake bottoms or flowing into lakes attract fish, especially during very cold and very hot weather. The nearly constant 45- to 55-degree F springwater provides most fish with a comfortable temperature. Fishfinders are valuable tools for locating these areas and fish in large deep rivers, lakes, and oceans.

If fish do not strike your flies as quickly as you expect them to, have patience and keep your mind tuned to reading and studying the water. Change flies and methods, and try different areas. Fish do not feed constantly, and there will be periods each day when they seem asleep, and other times when they will be outright aggressive. Anglers often find their greatest satisfaction and pleasure in using their skill and wit to catch the fish that is the most reluctant to take the artificial fly.

THE BIOLOGY

OF FISH

Fish are born, live, feed, and reproduce in a different medium than ours. To fly fish successfully for them you must understand their world of water and how they function in it.

▼

Fish live as cold-blooded animals. Unlike us, their metabolism is continually affected by the temperature of the medium in which they live and breathe. As warm-blooded animals, we maintain a constant body temperature (98.6 degrees F). Our metabolism and activity can remain relatively constant over the four seasons. Because fish are cold-blooded and cannot keep their body temperature and metabolism constant, their level of activity is continually affected by the seasonal temperature variations of the water.

There is a temperature range of about 20 to 25 degrees F in which most fish metabolize well. When the water is colder or warmer than this range, they usually become sluggish or dormant, even dying if temperatures drop too low or rise too high above their ideal. To catch these fish as they are feeding actively and full of fighting energy, you must choose the right season and water temperatures for the species you wish to catch. There are four general groups of fish classified as to their temperature comfort zones.

- Cold-water fish, 40 to 65 degrees F

- Cool-water fish, 50 to 75 degrees F

- Warm-water fish, 60 to 85 degrees F

- Tropical fish, 65 to 90 degrees F

Water with temperatures in the middle ranges of each of these groups is where you will usually find the species you wish to fish for most actively feeding.

WATER TEMPERATURE COMFORT ZONES

Water Temperature Zones fish are most active. These ranges may vary 5 to 10° due to adaptation of species in some borderline ares.

Cold Water	
Trout	45 to 65 °F
Char	40 to 60 °F
Salmon	45 to 65 °F
Grayling	40 to 60 °F
Whitefish	50 to 70 °F

Cool Water	
Pike	50 to 70 °F
Musky	50 to 70 °F
Pickerel	55 to 75 °F
Walleye	55 to 75 °F
Yellow Perch	55 to 75 °F
Striped Bass	50 to 70 °F
Bluefish	50 to 70 °F
Smallmouth Bass	55 to 75 °F

Warm and Tropical	
Largemouth Bass	60 to 80 °F
Crappie	60 to 80 °F
White Bass	55 to 75 °F
Sunfishes	55 to 80 °F
Catfish	55 to 80 °F
Carp	55 to 80 °F
Redfish	55 to 75 °F
Tarpon	60 to 85 °F
Snook	60 to 85 °F
Bonefish	70 to 85 °F

When the water temperature dips lower than these ranges, fish tend to slow down in activity and feeding, and are likely to stay in deeper (warmer) water as surface temperatures get colder.

Surface feeding is most likely when water temperatures are in the upper ranges of these comfort zones; fish will also tend to stay in shallower water at these times. When water temperatures become significantly warmer than the comfort zones, fish usually become more or less inactive or lethargic. This is because warmer water contains less oxygen.

At lower temperatures, water holds more oxygen, so at the upper temperature limits fish often swim to deeper, colder water or to sources of colder water, such as springs and cooler tributary creeks. If these are unavailable, fish move to areas of maximum aeration, such as waterfalls, rapids, riffles, or windy surface areas. If these are unavailable, fish will gulp air at the water's surface. This, however, is a last resort before a fish suffocates and dies.

SEASONS

The four seasons affect a fish's activity in a number of ways. Winter usually is the period of least activity. Summer may also be a less active time because the water is often too warm. In the spring or fall, when water temperatures are closest to ideal for them, most fish have a mating, and spawning, season. Just before and during spawning season, fish are most easily located and caught on flies.

Each season, various species of fish move and search for the most comfortable water temperature. Water is much denser than air, so it changes temperature much more slowly than air. Fish may seek shallow, sunlit water in cold seasons or swim deep to escape the chill of a cold storm or intense heat of a long hot, dry

STREAM-WATER STRUCTURES
Aquatic vegetation, large boulders, rubble, tree limbs, roots, and overhead trees make ideal hiding and feeding structures for fish such as trout and smallmouth bass.

spell. As they do this, they also try to find those areas where food and oxygen are plentiful—just as you would in your own comfort zone.

Fish also need shelter and protection: places to rest and hide from their enemies. These may be water structures, such as aquatic plants, boulders, holes, deeper water, and the like. Many fish species use these same areas to locate and gather or ambush live foods.

To find and catch fish consistently, you must locate areas where the right temperature and oxygen conditions combine with good structural environment to hide the fish and hold ample amounts of their food. Each species of fish has a specific pattern of requirements you should know and watch for. The challenge is to pick the right food imitation and skillfully present it in these "holding" areas to make the fish think it is alive and easy to catch.

FISH SENSES: THE KEY TO GOOD IMITATIONS

Fish locate, inspect, and eat natural foods using their senses of sight, hearing, smell, and taste/touch. There are two major types of fish: **predators** and **scavengers.** Predators catch most of their food alive, while scavengers usually eat inanimate or dead foods. Each type uses a highly developed set of senses to locate foods and avoid or escape their predators. Both types can be caught on flies that correctly imitate these preferred foods.

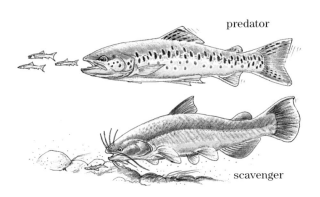

Predator fish feed primarily on live animal food. Scavenger fish feed primarily on dead animal forms and vegetation.

Sight

Sight is a well-developed sense in most fish, especially those that are predators. Fish see either binocularly (with both eyes forward) or monocularly (one on each side of their heads), and have good close vision. Because of water clarity restrictions, fish have no need to see more than 20 or 30 feet away. They have good color vision as well, and most species have excellent night vision. Predators rely mostly on sight while scavengers use it as a secondary sense for locating foods.

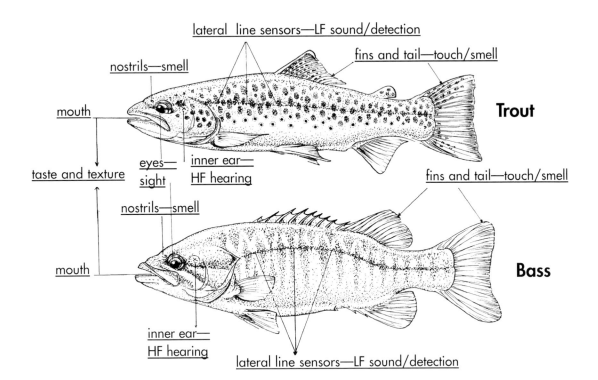

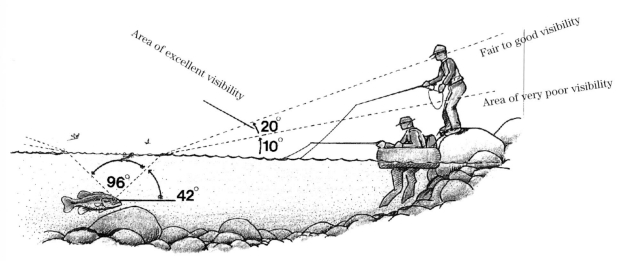

This diagram shows how fish see above the surface at various light-ray refractions. At 10 degrees off horizontal, fish see very poorly, especially on dark or very windy days. At 20 degrees off horizontal, fish vision is fair if light is good and the surface is calm. At over 20 degrees, fish see very well under most conditions.

Hearing

Fish have highly developed dual hearing systems. The ears in their heads intercept high-frequency vibrations (200 to 800 cycles per second), and some can hear from 30 to 2,000 CPS. This form of hearing is much like our own except not as wide in range.

Fish also have a lateral-line hearing organ on each side of their bodies that picks up low-frequency vibrations, 200 to 15 CPS. This lateral line, which runs from behind the head to the base of the tail, is a series of tiny drumlike membranes with nerve ends that run from each to the spinal cord. With the lateral line fish can detect the size, speed, and direction of movement in the water of an object—such as another fish, a snake, a mink, or a fisherman. They use this line to detect food as well as enemies.

Since sounds travel faster and more efficiently in water, fish rely on this dual hearing system almost as much as or sometimes even more than on sight to detect food and escape dangers, especially at times of low visibility.

Smell

Fish have a highly developed sense of smell that is much better than ours and surpasses even that of a bird dog or bloodhound. Both predator and scavenger fish identify foods by odor, but the scavengers use smell as their primary sense to detect and locate food. Predators, on the other hand, use smell more to confirm food they have located by sight or hearing.

Taste/Touch

On the surfaces of their bodies, fins, and mouths, fish have sensors that can taste and feel their foods. These are more or less secondary senses used after the potential food is located or captured. For instance, a fish might locate your fly and rub its body across it or bite it to determine if it is real food or fake.

Often, when a fish uses these sensors, it appears that the fish has missed the fly when, in reality, it has touched and tasted it and in an instant rejected it because it did not feel or taste right. This is why you must react to a strike quickly, before the fish can recognize your fly as a fake and reject it. An effective imitation must look, sound, feel, and taste like real food to a fish. This is the fascinating challenge of fly fishing.

Predator fish are the most aggressive eaters and thus usually easier to catch on flies than are the less aggressive scavengers. Scavengers, on the other hand, are more easily spooked than most predators. They are also often more selective feeders, and so there is quite a challenge in finding (or creating) a fly that smells and tastes almost natural and then precisely presenting that fly to the fish. Because of this selectivity and their shy nature, most scavenger fish, once hooked, quickly panic and try to flee and escape in a fury of fast, strong runs. In my opinion, scavenger fish are worthy sportfish, truly as much fun for fly fishing as predator fish.

NATURAL FOODS 6 FOR FISH

Wherever fish live, there is a natural food chain. Knowing food sources, imitating them with flies, and fishing them to fool and catch fish are the marks of a good fly fisher. A basic knowledge of streams, lakes, marshes, estuaries, oceans, and the fish foods they hold is important.

▼

Unpolluted freshwater streams and lakes usually produce abundant fish foods. The major fish foods are aquatic insects, small fish, crustaceans, aquatic invertebrates, terrestrial insects, small mammals, small reptiles and other invertebrates, and aquatic plants.

AQUATIC INSECTS

Aquatic insects live a major part of their life cycles underwater. Their life cycles are generally one year, but in some groups life cycles are as short as two months or as long as four years. These insects provide fish with convenient year-round opportunities to feed on the immature nymph forms and the adults. Because of their abundance and vulnerability, they are often favored by fish such as trout, bass, or panfish, and so are important for the fly fisher to imitate. They are seldom important in saltwater fishing.

The most abundant aquatic insects are mayflies, stoneflies, caddisflies, midges, damselflies, and dragonflies. The life cycle for these insects include an aquatic nymph stage, which eventually emerges onto the water's surface and hatches into a winged adult insect stage. These adults, which live only a few hours, days, or weeks, mate and lay their eggs on the water (egg stage) and then die.

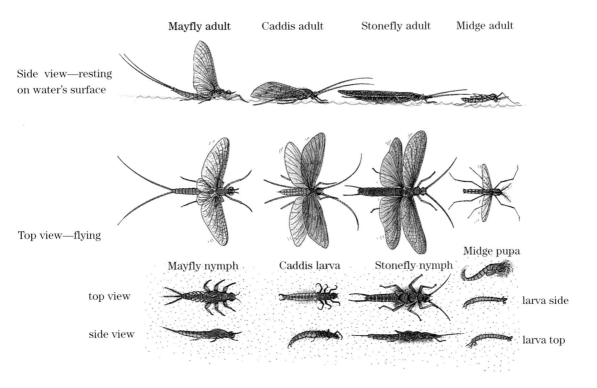

Mayfly adult   Caddis adult   Stonefly adult   Midge adult

Side view—resting on water's surface

Top view—flying

Mayfly nymph   Caddis larva   Stonefly nymph   Midge pupa

top view

side view   larva side

larva top

Four major aquatic insects that fish most often eat and fly fishers imitate with flies.

It was the desire to imitate these aquatic insects that initially stimulated the sport of fly fishing. A large number of standard fly designs are imitations of aquatic insects. Matching and fishing aquatic insects is still the most captivating method of fly fishing for trout, grayling, char, bass, and panfish.

Mayflies (Ephemeroptera) are a large, very important group of delicate, harmless aquatic insects that live in streams and lakes. The life cycle consists of egg, nymph, and adult stages. The nymph, which feeds and grows beneath the surface from periods of a few months to a year or two years, swims to the surface when mature and hatches into the first adult stage, the dun. The winged dun, an air breather, flies off the water's surface, leaving its nymphal skin behind. It conceals itself in the waterside terrestrial structures (trees, weeds, rocks, or bushes). The dun, after a short period—minutes to a day or so—sheds another skin and changes into the more vividly colored, sexually mature adult stage called the **spinner.** Spinners form a swarm and fly near or over the water and mate in the air. The females immediately fly down to the water's surface and lay their eggs on or below the surface. Both males and females die shortly after this activity.

Mayfly adult

Mayfly imitation

Mayfly nymph

Mayfly nymph imitation

The mayfly is the hallmark of the origin of fly fishing.

INSECT SIZE AND SEASON

Northern Hemisphere

AQUATIC INSECTS

January to March: small sizes (18 to 26) of midges, mayflies, caddisflies, and stoneflies.

March to June: small to medium sizes (12 to 18) of mayflies, caddisflies, midges, and stoneflies.

June to August: large and small sizes (4 to 24) of caddisflies, mayflies, damselflies, stoneflies, midges, and dragonflies.

August to October: small and medium sizes (16 to 24) of mayflies, caddisflies, and midges.

October to December: small sizes (18 to 26) of midges, mayflies, and caddisflies.

TERRESTRIAL INSECTS

Generally in small sizes (16 to 18) beginning around April,

An adult is most recognizable by its large, upright, sail-shaped wings (at rest); long, round, slender, tapering body; and two or three tails. Nymphs have sets of gills on the sides and top of the abdominal segments and one pair of wing pads on their thorax.

Stoneflies (Plecoptera) are harmless aquatic insects that are generally large and live in very pure, well-aerated streams. They have a life cycle very similar to that of mayflies. The adult is best identified by two large pairs of wings, which at rest are folded or rolled around the top sides of the body, giving the insect an almost sticklike appearance. It has two distinctive large antennae and two distinctive tails, very widely separated.

Stonefly nymphs vary widely in size, color, and shape, according to species and age. Nymphs are best identified by their two distinctive wing cases (pads), two tails and antennae, and a fuzzy, light-colored gill filaments under and between their six legs.

Most stonefly nymphs emerge by crawling out of the water onto the stream shoreline. Smaller stoneflies, sizes 12 to 16 ($^1/_2$ to $^3/_4$ inch) often swim to the water's surface to emerge.

Caddisflies (Trichoptera) are a very widely distributed group of harmless, mothlike, lake and stream insects. They have a four-stage life cycle: egg, larva, pupa, and adult. The life cycle generally lasts one year. From the **egg,** a **larva** is produced. This grubwormlike larva lives at the bottom of the water.

Three common forms of cased caddis larvae

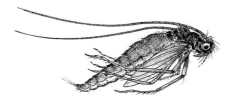

Emergent caddis pupa

Many species of caddisfly larvae construct a case in which they live. These cases are made uniquely according to species from glue and silklike filament in combination with aquatic plant pieces, sand grains, or terrestrial plant parts. The cases are for protection and camouflage. Along the bottom, they resemble short, sticklike structures.

The larva develops into the third stage, the **pupa,** which is very similar to the cocoon of a butterfly or moth. The larva seals its case to begin pupation. This stage generally lasts a few weeks. Then the pupa, now very different physically from the larva, cuts out of its case; swims, rises, or crawls to the surface; and hatches into the **adult** caddisfly.

Adults live several days to several weeks, during which time they mate and lay eggs on or below the water's surface.

Adults are best distinguished from the three other major aquatic insects discussed by their tentlike or mothlike wing shape when at rest. Many appear opaque, fuzzy, mottled, and heavily veined. Caddisflies have two very long antennae and no distinctive tails on a modestly sized body.

The larva has a rather bare, light-colored abdomen with considerable gill filaments on its lower side. It has no visible wing pads on its darker thorax and no easily visible antennae or tails.

increasing in a variety of sizes steadily to early September, then decreasing in number but not size until fall and winter freezes. The crawling ants and beetles are first to appear in spring. Crawling and flying ants, moths, bees, flies, small and large beetles, inchworms, spiders, small crickets, and grasshoppers appear from late spring to midsummer. Flying and crawling ants, small beetles, various sizes of grasshoppers and crickets, leafhoppers, spiders, bees, wasps, caterpillars, and spiders appear from late summer until the first frost of fall.

NOTE: Aquatic adult insects and immature and adult terrestrial insects are most frequently imitated with floating flies. Immature aquatic insects (nymphs, larvae, pupae) are generally imitated with sinking flies.

The pupa has six long, skinny legs, wing pads at the side or lower part of its midsection (thorax), and two very distinctive antennae. A good way to study pupae is to pick their sealed cases off the bottom structures and carefully open them to remove the delicate developing insects.

Midges (Diptera) are a very widely distributed and immensely abundant group of aquatic insects. Some members of the Diptera family, such as mosquitoes, blackflies, and deerflies, are biting bloodsuckers in their adult form. Midges have a very similar but usually shorter life cycle than caddisflies. They are generally very small insects, seldom exceeding ¼ inch in length.

The very important, harmless, mosquitolike midge adult is identified by its one pair of wings, which are smaller than its body and positioned flat on top and to each side of the body at rest. It has three pairs of very long, skinny legs. Males have two very large, plumelike antennae, but no tails.

The larvae are very simple, slender, segmented worms with no distinctively clear head, body, or tail. The pupae are similar in color to the larvae but have a much fatter head-thorax section. Close magnification will show gill plumes on the head and tail and folded legs and wings under the head-thorax section.

TERRESTRIAL INSECTS

Terrestrial insects—those insects that are born and spend their immature and mature stages on land—are a second major insect food source for many fresh-

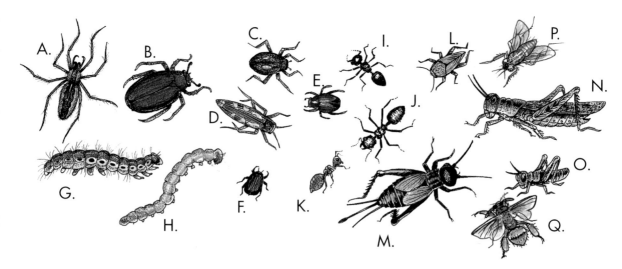

These are the terrestrial insects most important to imitate:

A. Spiders   B, C, D, E, F. Beetles G. Caterpillars   H. Inchworms I, J, K. Ants L. Leafhoppers (Jassids)
M. Crickets N. Grasshoppers (mature) O. Grasshoppers (immature) P. Houseflies   Q. Bees

water fish. This is especially so in warmer latitudes and, through the summer months, in colder parts of North America.

Fish feed on terrestrial insects that accidentally fall on the water during flight, during mating swarms, or from overhanging plants. Wind, rain, cold snaps, floods, drought, crop harvesting, and similar activities often create conditions that force terrestrial insects to become water-trapped. Some sink slowly, but most will float low in the water's surface film. Most terrestrial fly imitations are low-floating designs.

The important terrestrial insects to imitate are ants, beetles, grasshoppers, leafhoppers, crickets, caterpillars (worms), wasps, moths, bees, and spiders. Terrestrial insects usually become more abundant and larger after aquatic insects decline in numbers and slow down in activity, around midsummer and into the fall months. Terrestrial insect activity slows or ceases with freezing weather.

CRUSTACEANS

This is an important large group of natural aquatic fish foods that are similar to both aquatic insects and fish in their movements, shapes, and habits. They are widely distributed. The most important crustaceans for the freshwater fly fisher to imitate are scuds (freshwater shrimp), sow bugs, and crayfish. All three of these crawl along the bottom structures of lakes and streams. The scud and crayfish can swim erratically and rapidly backward if fleeing from a fish. Sow bugs, however, crawl along the bottom and are feeble swimmers at best.

Saltwater crustaceans important to imitate are various crabs, shrimp, and crayfish. Each of these can crawl and swim.

All species have a simple life cycle lasting one to several years, in which they seasonally increase in size. Like most other cold-blooded creatures, crustaceans are most active and abundant during the milder seasons. They are imitated by using wet flies and modified streamer designs. In still water, cast the imitation, allow it to sink nearly to the bottom, and strip it back toward you. In flowing water, strip it across and downstream.

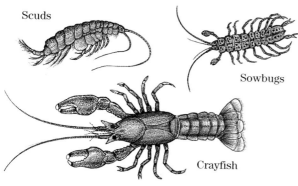

Scuds

Sowbugs

Crayfish

These are important crustaceans to imitate.

OTHER INVERTEBRATES

Earthworms and aquatic worms, aquatic leeches, and snails make up

Aquatic worm   *Swimming leech*

an assortment of fish foods that varies in importance depending on their abundance compared to the other major foods already described. Knowledge of their existence, life cycles, actions, sizes, and colors will—if used to properly create and fish imitations—enable the fly fisher to make good catches.

MINNOWS

Minnow is the name used by anglers to indicate mature small fish or immature large fish that other fish feed on. Minnows are sometimes called forage or baitfish. Like aquatic insects, they are important and abundant fish foods in fresh water. Minnows are extremely important in salt water, as well.

Their life cycles, usually several years long, expose them daily to predator fish that ambush, chase, and eat them. Minnows are imitated by streamers and wet flies.

Fish eat a wide range of minnows. Generally, practical fly-fishing sizes are $1/2$ to 8 inches long. They vary from natural colors to bright attractor colors. Minnows are found in all water areas from top to bottom, but usually choose an area specific to their species. For example, shad and shiners live in clear, open water, chub and dace near underwater structures, and sculpin and suckers on the bottom.

Minnow imitations are usually fished to imitate panic or distress. This action suggests vulnerability and stimulates attack by predator fish.

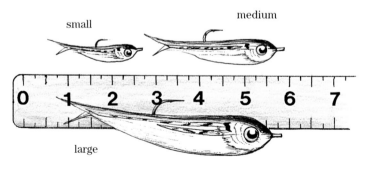

Most minnow species are 1 to 6 inches in length and can be imitated with three streamer-fly sizes.

To sample most fish foods that swim, crawl, or burrow in a stream, use a fine screen seine to capture them.

SAMPLING FISH FOODS

It's a good practice, before you fly fish a water, to observe what fish foods are available there. This is done by watching the air, shorelines, and water for naturals and by catching air, land, and aquatic foods with various capture nets. A few minutes of sampling live foods will pay excellent dividends when it comes to choosing the right imitations.

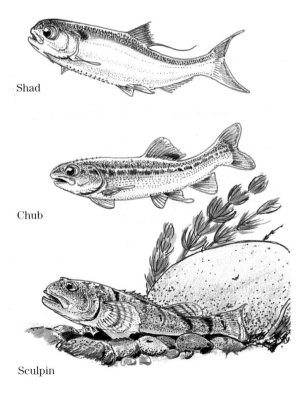

Shad

Chub

Sculpin

THE ECOLOGY OF FISHERIES

Food chain is the term used to describe the sequence of feeding from the simple plants and animals through the most complex forms. Each more complex form feeds upon the lesser forms. The least complex forms feed on the decomposing matter of the higher forms, thus completing the endless food chain. The experienced fly fisher recognizes an excellent fishery by the food chain. Water lacking a good food chain provides poor fishing or no fishing. If fishing is poor or changes from excellent to poor, it is a strong indication of larger problems in the environment.

As a sportsman, you have an obligation to look after the environment. You

Three major minnow types: Shad, found in open water; Chub, found near underwater structures; Sculpin, are bottom-dwelling.

may do so in many ways, such as by picking up litter, taking care not to damage shore or bottom, reporting pollution and game violations, cooperating with landowners, writing letters to support important wildlife management projects, donating to wildlife and conservation-preservation causes, volunteering to work on conservation projects, or releasing fish. Such investments will bring great dividends to you and future generations.

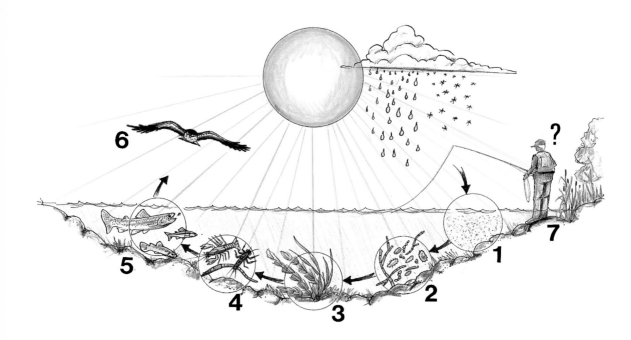

A food chain is driven by sunlight, oxygen, carbon, and water.

1. Dissolved nutrients 2. Algae and diatoms 3. Aquatic plants

4. Invertebrates 5. Fish 6. Air and land predators 7. Man—What roll are we playing in the conservative use and preservation of a successful food chain on the waters? We are just as dependent on clean water as the other food chain members.

7 FISH MADE FOR FLY FISHING

Fly fishing, especially when complemented by innovative and creative fly tying, is a fascinating method that provides almost limitless opportunity to catch almost *any* species of fish. You must be able to identify the fish; determine what it eats or will strike, and where, how, and when it will strike; and then tempt the fish into accepting your chosen fly.

▼

Some fish, such as trout, salmon, bass, and bonefish, are classic fly-fishing quarry called **gamefish.** Others are thought to be of lesser sport. This is an arbitrary classification, however, and you will be better off making your own judgments here. You might be pleasantly surprised. I feel that any fish is more fun to catch fly fishing than with any other fishing method. Actually, I enjoy catching them all . . . and I predict you will also.

FRESHWATER FISH

TROUT (Trout Family)

Trout are widely distributed cold-water stream and lake fish, and are the most traditional and popular fly-fishing quarry. In fact, trout probably are the main reason fly fishing was first conceived, and they have been the fish most sought after by fly fishers. The most common and widely fished species are rainbow trout, brown trout, cutthroat trout, and (more rare) golden trout. (The brook trout is actually a char, and is dealt with in the next section.)

In the Northern Hemisphere, most unpolluted freshwater streams and lakes that have average summertime temperatures of 50 to 60 degrees F and that seldom

Top: Brown trout
Bottom: Rainbow

reach 70 degrees F will likely have trout living in them. Trout are sleek, strong, fast, and beautifully colored fish. They feed aggressively on a wide variety of natural foods, and can be enticed to strike many natural or attractor-patterned flies. Trout feed most actively in rising or stable water temperatures of 50 to 60 degrees F. They feed principally by sight, either on or below the surface. Most prefer to eat live small insects, crustaceans, and minnows. There are many popular fly designs to imitate these foods.

Trout average 8 to 12 inches ($\frac{1}{2}$ pound) but 15- to 28-inch or larger (2 to 8-plus pounds) fish are regularly caught on flies. Take great care to release trout properly so that they may live to be caught again, or to spawn and provide the valuable breeding stock necessary to ensure future fishing.

Char (Trout Family)

Char are a widely distributed group of troutlike fish that inhabit cold and very cold waters of North America. Even more so than trout, they require very clean, clear, and cold lake or stream environments. Char are beautiful, vividly colored, strong, aggressive, and active fish. They feed on aquatic insects, minnows, fish eggs, aquatic worms, leeches, and crustaceans, and are generally thought to be more gullible than trout. Char prefer to feed in water of 40 to 55 degrees F.

The most popular species of true char are brook trout, arctic char, Dolly Varden, lake trout, and Sunapee trout. The splake is a hybrid char of brook- and lake-trout parentage. Brook trout are much more like true trout in their ranges and habits than other char. The other chars are larger-water, deeper-feeding min-

Brook trout (char)

now eaters in general, so minnow imitations work best. Char that will hit flies range widely in size from 8 inches to 20 pounds. The deep, cold-water-living lake trout often run larger in size. They are not, however, the best char for fly fishing, because they are usually found very deep in a lake and are hard to reach by casting flies. Char, like trout, should be harvested sparingly.

Grayling (Trout Family)

A beautiful, delicate, relatively rare, troutlike cold-water fish that is highly prized by North American fly fishers, the grayling has a distinctive, large, sail-fishlike dorsal fin. It requires very pure, cold, clear, lake or stream water. Most good grayling fishing is found in the Montana and Wyoming Rockies and in

Grayling

northwestern Canada and Alaska. Grayling feed predominantly on active insects but will also feed on crustaceans and small minnows. Smaller flies, especially dry flies, are most effective.

Grayling average 8 to 14 inches but grow as large as 4 pounds, especially in Alaska. They prefer to feed in water of 45 to 55 degrees F. Grayling are very active but not powerful fighters.

Landlock Salmon (Trout Family)

Landlocks are believed by many authorities to have evolved from Atlantic salmon that were landlocked, perhaps thousands of years ago. They are some-what smaller than Atlantic ocean salmon but every bit as beautiful, streamlined, fast, and hard-fighting. Land-locks occur naturally in the rivers and lakes of Maine and southeastern Canada and have been successfully introduced to a few other northeastern states and other sections of Canada,

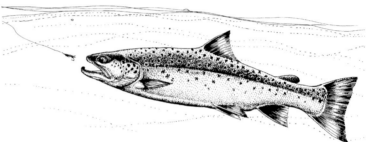

A landlocked salmon taking a wet fly.

as well as South America. They feed principally on minnows and aquatic insects and are aggressive surface and subsurface fly strikers.

Atlantic Salmon (Trout Family)

On the Atlantic Coast, only the Atlantic salmon is native, and it is second only to trout in traditional popularity with fly fishers. In fact, in North American rivers, sportfishing is limited to using flies to catch these magnificent fish as they enter the rivers from May to October for their spawning runs.

Although Atlantic salmon are thought not to feed once they return to fresh water to spawn, they strike wet, dry, and streamer salmon flies very well. As Atlantic salmon make their return journey to the ocean the following spring they are known as black salmon or kelts. These fish feed voraciously on spring-spawning smelt and other minnows and aggressively strike large, colorful streamer flies. Salmon range from 3 to 8 pounds (grilse) and 9 to 40 pounds for mature fish. Good conservation practices should always be used with these beautiful fish, for their stocks are threatened.

Atlantic salmon often jump completely out of the water when hooked.

Pacific Salmon (Trout Family)

There are five abundant species of Pacific salmon: chinook (or king), coho, silver, sockeye, pink, and chum. They are fine gamefish, but less popular with the traditional cold-water fly fisher than trout, Atlantic salmon, or char. Pacific salmon spawn once and die, whereas the Atlantic salmon may spawn more than once during its lifetime. Neither type of salmon eats once it returns to fresh water to spawn but will strike a wide variety of surface and subsurface attractor flies. All salmon are strong fighters. They average from 3 to 10 pounds for

chum and sockeye, 8 to 20 pounds for coho, and 12 to 40 for chinook. Some chinook exceed 60 pounds. In the past few decades, many Pacific salmon and some Atlantic salmon have been successfully introduced to larger freshwater lake systems, such as the Great Lakes in the United States and Canada, as well as

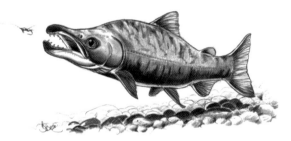

Pacific salmon take attractor wet flies best.

limited areas in the Southern Hemisphere including Argentina, Chile, and New Zealand.

Steelhead (Trout Family)

The steelhead is a unique rainbow trout that has adapted to a sea or large lake residence like salmon, and requires a temporary spawning run into connecting rivers. After spawning, steelhead return to the ocean or lake. Many feel that steelhead are equaled only by Atlantic salmon in their desirability as a large, strong, high-leaping, long-running freshwater fish to catch on a fly rod. They are most abundant in the coastal rivers from California to Alaska and in the Great Lakes. Steelhead average 4 to 8 pounds and often exceed 20 pounds in these areas. They do feed a little during

Steelhead

their upstream and downstream migrations and will strike both natural and attractor surface and subsurface flies.

Sea Trout (Trout Family)

Sea trout, or coasters, are names often used for trout that live in the sea and, like salmon and steelhead, swim up connecting rivers to spawn. Most common are brown trout, cutthroat, rainbow, and char (brook trout and Dolly Varden). Because of their sea vitality, all are usually larger and significantly stronger than their resident freshwater counterparts.

Largemouth, Smallmouth, and Spotted (Kentucky) Bass (Sunfish Family)

Bass are found in warm and cool water. They are strong, handsome, amazingly adaptive, and aggressive, and almost always willing to take a fly. They prefer freshwater and brackish-water lakes and slower streams that are relatively unpolluted and have an average summer temperature range of 65 to 80 degrees F. Most North American fresh waters that are not trout fisheries will be bass fisheries.

Bass are opportunistic and feed aggressively on all types of insects, crustaceans, minnows, amphibians, reptiles, and mammals. They are less selective and generally prefer larger foods than do trout. Bass can be solitary or found in small, loose schools. They prefer to ambush live surface and subsurface foods along shorelines or near open-water structures such as large boulders, aquatic plants, fallen trees, or boat docks. They feed most actively in rising or stable water temperatures of 55 to 80 degrees F.

There are three popular species of bass: **smallmouth, largemouth,** and **spotted (Kentucky)** bass. They average about 1 pound or 12 inches, but it is not unusual to catch 2- to 10-pound bass on flies.

Smallmouth bass are closer to trout in their habitat preference, often inhabiting cool water. They are generally more popular with fly fishers because they are such tenacious fighters. The spotted and largemouth bass, however, are also fine fly-rod fish. All three strike hard, jump frequently, and fight a strong close-quarters battle.

Streamer flies that imitate shad are effective for largemouth bass.

Smallmouth bass are spectacular jumpers when hooked on surface floating flies.

Bluegill (Sunfish Family)

Bluegill are the most popular and abundant panfish in North America's cool and warm waters. They normally inhabit the same waters as bass, but in far

Blue gill will eagerly strike small surface flies.

greater numbers. Bluegill are sassy, quick, strong, and very aggressive. They feed on or below the surface on live or dead insects, crustaceans, and minnows. They are sight feeders. Their small size and tiny mouths make it necessary for them to feed mostly on small foods. Flies from size 6 to 16, or 1 to $1/2$ inch long, are best.

Similar sunfish, such as common sunfish, long ear, yellow-breasted sunfish, red ear, green sunfish, rock bass, and pumpkinseed usually inhabit the same waters as bluegill and bass. All will strike similar types of flies and, like bluegill, they are usually very abundant. Most sunfish average 5 to 6 inches in length and occasionally grow to 1 pound or more. They are wonderful sport and convenient fish for practicing fly fishing.

Crappie (Sunfish Family)

A very abundant and widely distributed cool- and warm-water panfish, the crappie is usually present in the same waters as bass and bluegill, but generally prefers deeper, calmer water. Crappie are school fish that feed aggressively subsurface on small minnows, aquatic insects, and some crustaceans. They are usually found hiding and feeding beside and under various submerged structures, such as weed beds, reeds, dead trees, boat docks, or rock ledges. Crappie are both daytime and nighttime feeders.

There are two crappie species: white and black. The white crappie is generally more abundant in the South and Midwest and is a bit larger than the black. Blacks strike a fly more aggressively, fight a bit more, and do not form such large schools. Crappie average about 8 inches long and weigh between $1/2$ pound and 1 pound. But specimens are regularly caught, especially during shallow-water spawning, that may weigh $2^1/2$ pounds or more.

White Bass (Bass Family)

White bass are an extremely abundant school panfish found in warm, cool, and cold waters. They prefer larger lakes and rivers rich with minnows and insects. White bass move almost constantly, feeding at all depths. They are aggressive and will strike streamers, nymphs, and top-water bugs. They fight extremely hard for their size, which averages about $3/4$ pound to $2^1/2$ pounds. They also have a short life span of only three to four years.

White Perch (Temperate Bass Family)

White perch are abundant schooling fish that average $3/4$ to 1 pound. They inhabit mostly northeastern and eastern seaboard state lakes and larger rivers that are classed as cool- or warm-water environments. Like their black-striped cousins, the white bass and yellow bass, they can be caught on small subsurface flies that imitate favorite foods such as minnows, aquatic worms, and aquatic insects. They are aggressive fly strikers, and fight well. White perch, like white bass, make midspring spawning runs up rivers and lake inlet streams. At this time they are easiest to locate and reach with flies. During the summer and fall they school and stay off reefs and deep lake points, feeding most aggressively early and late each day.

Yellow Perch (Perch Family)

A relatively abundant cool-water panfish, the yellow perch prefers lakes but also inhabits some streams that usually are considered bass or marginal trout waters. They prefer to feed on subsurface and bottom aquatic insects, crustaceans, worms, and small minnows. They strike best on small flies fished slow and

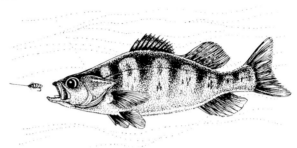

Yellow perch prefer subsurface flies that imitate minnows and aquatic insects.

deep. Perch average about 10 inches ($^1/_2$ pound) and some run as large as 2 pounds. They are fun to catch but are not particularly spectacular fighters.

Walleye and Sauger (Perch Family)

Other common names for these fish are walleye pike, jack fish, and pickerel. Walleye and sauger are very popular cool- to cold-water schooling fish. They are widely distributed, living in clean, hard-bottomed, deep lakes and streams. Much like crappie, they make up in beauty what they lack in hard-fighting character. Most are nocturnal, subsurface feeders.

Walleye are predominantly minnow and leech feeders but occasionally feed on aquatic insects, amphibians, crustaceans, and worms. They average about 1 pound but 3- to 7-pound fly-caught walleye are not uncommon.

Northern Pike (Pike Family)

Pike are fairly widely distributed cool- and cold-water lake and stream fish that are found mostly in the northern United States, Canada, and southern Alaska. They are strong, very aggressive fish that prefer to ambush their food from near

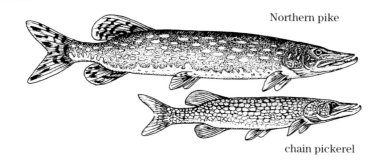

Northern pike

chain pickerel

The Northern pike is larger, but the pickerel hits a fly faster, harder, and fights more.

shore and bottom structures. They feed mostly on other fish, amphibians, crustaceans, mammals, and birds in water of 45 to 65 degrees F. As fly-rod fish, there has not been nearly enough said—they are truly as exciting or more so than bass or trout.

Pike are alligatorlike in appearance, and that may discourage some fly fishers from appreciating them. They are frequently caught accidentally on bass flies or large trout flies. They average 20 inches and about 3 pounds, but often weigh as much as 15 to 30 pounds.

Muskellunge (Muskie) (Pike Family)

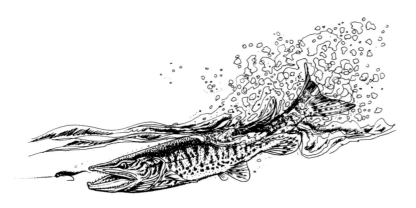

A muskie, the tiger of freshwater fish, are outstanding to catch on a fly.

Muskie are large, somewhat rare, beautifully and vividly colored pikelike fish that are less widely distributed than northern pike but live in the same lake or stream conditions. Muskie are rarely caught on flies. However, they present a great challenge to the fly fisher because of their very large size (8 to 25 pounds), high intelligence, and wonderful fighting qualities. They make long runs and jump much more than pike. A stream muskie over 30 inches caught on a top-water fly is probably a more rare and highly prized fly-rod trophy than any other freshwater gamefish.

Chain Pickerel (Pike Family)

This is a smaller pikelike fish in the same family as pike and muskie. Chain pickerel are much more widespread in streams and lakes of the East and South, and they are lightning-fast, vicious, hard-striking, surface and subsurface ambush feeders. Their surface strike is something to be experienced! They are strong fighters that frequently "tail-walk" the surface when hooked. They feed on minnows, crayfish, leeches, large insects, amphibians, and small mammals. They average 12 to 18 inches, and occasionally 2- to 6-pounders are caught on flies. Most bass flies work equally well for pickerel.

NOTE: These three pike family fish have rows of long, needle-sharp teeth. Fly fishers should us a heavy nylon monofilament bite tippet of 40- to 80-pound test or a wire tippet to prevent them from biting off the fly. Avoid any hand or finger contact with the insides of their mouths or their gill rakers or you'll probably suffer painful cuts and abrasions. There are several tools available made to remove flies safely from a pike's mouth.

Shad (Herring Family)

American shad

A group of abundant, delicate, silver, deep-bodied school fish, shad principally prefer cool-to-warm, fresh, brackish, and salt waters. Most of these fish, including hickory shad, gizzard shad, American shad, skipjack, and golden eye, will strike small, flashy, brightly colored attractor flies during their spring spawning runs up streams that flow into larger rivers, lakes, and oceans.

These fish are fast, strong fighters and generally willing leapers. They average from about 1 to 3 pounds, with some species running up to 5 or 6 pounds.

Carp (Minnow Family)

Carp

Carp are abundant, incredibly hardy, golden-colored scavenger fish that live in warm, cool, or cold waters. They will readily take flies that closely imitate their preferred natural foods of aquatic insects, aquatic worms, terrestrial plants, tree seeds or fruits, and aquatic vegetation. Taking them consistently on flies requires as high a degree of fly-fishing skill as does any fish you will encounter. Carp average 3 to 8 pounds and often exceed 20 pounds. Their careful, slow foraging on the surface and on the shallow bottom of clear lakes and slow-moving streams, with their small, sensitive mouths, makes them a real test for the fly fisher. Sight-casting to individual fish is the most consistent and fun way to catch carp on flies. Once hooked, they are beastly strong and stubborn fighters. Fly fishers discovering carp for the first time often compare them to bonefish, hence their affectionate name, the "poor man's bonefish."

Catfish (Catfish Family)

Principally warm- and cool-water scavenger fish, catfish are abundant in most slow-moving streams, ponds, and lakes. They feed mainly by smell and touch at night or in murky waters, and by sight in some situations. They can be caught on flies that imitate their favorite natural foods, such as minnows, crayfish, aquatic worms, larger aquatic and terrestrial insects, and terrestrial plant seeds

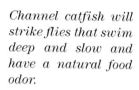

Channel catfish will strike flies that swim deep and slow and have a natural food odor.

and fruits. The channel, blue, and bullhead catfish are most easily caught on scented, slow, deep-fished flies during the day or on or near the surface at night. They average from 1 to 3 pounds, but several species grow to 20 or even 50 pounds. Catfish, especially the channel cat, are often hooked by fly fishers while fishing for bass and trout, convincing lucky fly fishers that they've hooked the biggest bass or trout in the fishery!

Gar (Gar Family)

An armor-plated, cool- and warm-water prehistoric fish with fiercely toothed jaws that would shame a pike or alligator, the gar is abundant in most lakes and streams of the Mississippi and Ohio river systems as well as all the southern states west to Texas. All three major species—short-nosed, long-nosed, and alligator gar—are aggressive minnow predators and will strike most flies that imitate them. But because of their excessive rows of teeth set in iron-hard jaws, it's nearly impossible to *hook* them. They are best caught on nylon-floss hookless streamers. The fine nylon floss tangles in their rows of teeth. Gar are fun to catch, but take extreme care not to touch their mouths or you will surely be cut or bitten.

SALTWATER FISH

In recent years, saltwater fly fishing has become very popular, especially for certain species that frequent coastlines, tidal rivers, and shallow bays or flats. Although saltwater fish exceeding 150 pounds have been taken on fly tackle, most saltwater fly fishing is for species weighing 2 to 25 pounds. Because living conditions in oceans are demanding and dangerous, most saltwater fish are several times faster and stronger than freshwater species of equal weight.

Bonefish (Bonefish Family)

Bonefish, also called the gray ghost and the silver fox, are silvery, sleek, torpedo-shaped, long-winded sprinters of shallow tropical flats. Extremely popular with saltwater fly fishers, bones average about 3 or 4 pounds and occasionally exceed 10 pounds. Hooked on a fly, they speed away and fight like a fish three times their weight! Bonefish can be caught on small subsurface flies that imitate favorite foods such as shrimp, crab, shellfish, worms, and minnows. Bonefish are hunted and eaten constantly by shark, barracuda, and birds of prey so they are nervous, very cautious fish, having only their hearing, eyesight, color, and swimming speed to protect themselves. They are hard to see and approach, and proper fly presentation is difficult. But when hooked, exciting, high-speed dashes make bonefish worth the effort. Bonefish are usually carefully released by sport anglers.

Tarpon (Tarpon Family)

The tarpon, the uncontested king of saltwater fly fishing, is one of the world's most beautiful and spectacular gamefish. The silver king is a tropical to subtropical fish, and prefers water temperatures above 70 degrees F.

Tarpon

Tarpon migrate north up the Atlantic Coast and Gulf of Mexico each spring and summer and back south to Central and South America in the fall and winter. Tarpon vary in weight from 1 to over 200 pounds; all sizes, when hooked, make wonderful high jumps and strong runs. They will hit almost any fly that imitates minnows, squid, crab, sea worms, or shrimp.

Tarpon have rough-lipped jaws, so you must use a heavy nylon bite tippet to prevent their wearing through the leader and escaping.

Because they are so special as gamefish, most tarpon are carefully released by sport anglers.

Ladyfish (Tarpon Family)

The ladyfish is a slender, silver, airborne flash of lightning when caught on light fly tackle, fighting far harder than its size would indicate—literally ripping the water with frequent leaps and long tail-walks. Ladyfish are quite common along the southern Atlantic Coast states, especially in Florida and along the western Gulf Coast. Ladyfish average about $1/2$ to 1 pound and grow to 5 or 6 pounds. They strike small, fast-retrieved surface and subsurface swimming flies that imitate minnows and shrimp. They are especially active at night around lights over the water in places where tidal flows are strong, such as boat and fishing docks, jetties, bridges, and tidal creek channels.

Redfish (Drum Family)

Redfish, or channel bass, are becoming very popular as a poor man's bonefish. They are both more abundant and more widely distributed than bonefish, ranging

Redfish

along the Atlantic Coast from Virginia to the Florida Keys to southern Texas and Mexico. Redfish prefer to cruise and feed along shallow coastal beaches, bays, flats, channel cuts, islands, keys, trawl ramps, and brackish-water lagoons and channels. Although they are splendid fly-fishing targets and are on average larger than bonefish—about 4 to 10 pounds, up to 30 pounds or more—they are not as spooky, selective, or hard-fighting as bonefish. What they lack in sophistication, they make up for in abundance, aggressiveness, size, and brute strength.

Redfish will aggressively and repeatedly strike surface and subsurface flies that imitate their favorite foods—crabs, shrimp, shellfish, minnows, and aquatic worms. Because redfish were almost wiped out by commercial and sportfishing and by environmental damage, most states have aggressive programs to restore them, with fishing restrictions such as closed seasons and strict limits; some areas even have stocking programs. Today, redfish are becoming much more abundant as a result of this concern. Most fly-caught redfish are released so that they will have an opportunity to spawn and increase the chances of restoring the fantastic redfishing of the past.

Weakfish (Drum Family)

Weakfish range from Massachusetts to Mexico along the Atlantic Coast. The two important species are the common weakfish and the better-known spotted weakfish or sea trout, so called because they have black spots similar to trout. The name *weakfish* refers to their tender mouths, which often tear when hooked.

Weakfish are great fly-rod fish. They are plentiful in shallow coastal waters, and eagerly strike surface and subsurface flies that imitate their favorite food, shrimp or minnows.

Sea trout like to feed in cool- and warm-water temperatures—60 to 85 degrees F—over grassy flats, jetties, beach lines, tidal channels, and river mouths.

The weakfish population has suffered a fate similar to those of the redfish and snook, with commercial netting and sportfishing pressure causing their numbers and size to dwindle in many areas. As more coastal states stop netting and restrict sportfishing, the weakfish should rebound, as have the striper, redfish, and snook.

Bluefish (Bluefish Family)

Bluefish are ravenous school fish that terrorize baitfish along the Atlantic Coast from Maine to Argentina. Their bloody feeding frenzies along surf lines, in bays, and at the mouths of tidal rivers have earned them the nickname "choppers"; they slash and devour any baitfish unlucky enough to get in their paths. Because

Bluefish

they feed and move almost constantly in salt water, they are extremely strong, fast fighters and excellent fly-rod fish.

Blues run from 2 to 20 pounds, and usually travel in age-group schools as they migrate north in the summer and south in the fall and winter. They prefer fast-moving surface and subsurface flies that imitate frightened schooling baitfish, shrimp, and squid.

Their rows of sharp cutting teeth make a wire bite tippet almost mandatory. Also, take care not to put your fingers inside a blue's mouth; the fish will bite you severely.

Striped Bass (Temperate Bass Family)

Striped bass are native to the Atlantic Coast of North America, but also have been successfully introduced to the West Coast from northern California to Washington State, and into many large inland freshwater lakes and rivers.

Striped bass are an exciting, strong, beautiful schooling fish that usually weigh from 2 to 30 pounds and can exceed 50 to 70 pounds. Their name, *striped bass*, or *stripers*, comes from the vivid horizontal rows of black stripes on their backs and sides, running from head to tail against a silvery background. Striped bass occur naturally in salt water, but to spawn they must swim up freshwater rivers, similar to salmon. Stripers also can live very well in large landlocked freshwater systems. Stripers readily strike subsurface and surface flies that imitate their favorite foods, such as sand eels, American eel, menhaden, smelt, shad, porgies, sculpin, aquatic worms, crabs, and shrimp. Because stripers are very tolerant of water temperatures—38 to 80 degrees F—they can be caught

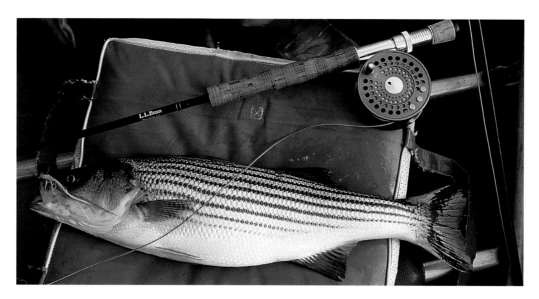

Striped bass

almost all year where they live.

In the last ten to fifteen years, stripers have made a remarkable comeback along the Atlantic Coast and tidal rivers due to strict seasons and limits on lengths and amounts anglers can harvest. Stripers are considered one of the finest fresh- and saltwater gamefish you can catch on a fly.

Mackerel (Tuna Family)

Mackerel are a group of streamlined, swift-swimming, razor-toothed, eating machines that travel in schools. They are found off both the Atlantic and Pacific Coasts of North America from Canada to Mexico. Most species of mackerel will strike any small subsurface fly that even remotely resembles minnows, squid, aquatic worms, shrimp, and so on. When the 1- to 2-pound fish are in a feeding school, it's often possible to catch two, three, or four at a time if you use that many flies on your leader.

Two larger mackerel species—the Sierra mackerel of Pacific Central America and the king mackerel, or kingfish, an Atlantic Coast species—grow considerably larger (5 to 30 pounds) than the more common and abundant smaller mackerel.

Snook (Snook Family)

Many feel that snook are second only to tarpon as the most perfect saltwater fish for the fly rodder. Snook are beautifully shaped and colored, extremely strong fighters and jumpers, and intelligent feeders. They average about 3 pounds and 18 inches, but frequently are caught from 5 to 20 pounds and occasionally to 30 pounds or more.

Snook range mostly from Florida's Atlantic coast to the Gulf of Mexico and south into Central America. They prefer to live around shallow-water structures such as oyster bars, mangroves, jetties, bridges, lagoons, tidal creeks, canals, and flats. Snook also will move into brackish- and freshwater bays to feed. They will strike surface and subsurface flies that imitate baitfish, shrimp, eels, swimming crabs, squid, and aquatic worms. The more skillful the fly angler is with accurate casts and precise retrieving, the more success he or she will have getting snook to strike. Snook are staging a comeback in Florida, with commercial netting now banned and with strict limitations on seasons, sizes, and amounts for sport anglers.

Barracuda (Barracuda Family)

Barracuda are a much underrated fly-fishing quarry—truly electrifying when hooked on a fly. They are lightning-bolt strikers, fast-swimming, long-jumping flashes of silver predator. Barracuda average about 3 to 10 pounds and frequently exceed 20 to 30 pounds. Their range is mostly along the Atlantic and Gulf coasts of Florida south to Central America. While most barracuda are probably caught by trolling in deep water or over wrecks using live bait, they are frequently found along beaches, islands, flats, channels, and mangroves. In these shallow areas, they will strike fast-moving surface and subsurface flies that imitate baitfish, especially long, slender ones that resemble the needlefish, their favorite food.

Barracuda have a set of teeth that would make any wolf envious. They can cut a fish in half with one bite, so take great care to keep your hands and legs safe when you are landing or unhooking a fish. You will need wire bite tippets to land these razor-toothed gamefish.

This rundown of fish that are favored by fly fishers is a list of only some of the popular and abundant fish that will strike flies. There are several dozen more freshwater species and at least a hundred more saltwater species targeted by fly fishers. A lot of the adventure, fun, and excitement of fly fishing is in catching unconventional as well as traditional fly-rod fish. To learn more about these fish and how to identify them, refer to A. J. McClane's *Field Guide to Freshwater Fishes of North America* and its companion book, *Guide to Saltwater Fishes of North America*.

SELECTING MATCHED FLY TACKLE FOR SPECIFIC SPECIES

TROUT: Light, small streams

Rod	7 to 8 feet, 3 to 5 weight, medium-fast action
Reel	Lightweight click-drag single action. Capacity: Up to DT 5F and 50 yards of backing
Backing	50 yards of 20-pound braided Dacron
Fly line	Matched to rod (3, 4, or 5) Double-taper floating
Leader	7 $\frac{1}{2}$- or 9-foot all-purpose knotless taper with 3X or 4X tip
Tippets	3X, 4X, 5X, 6X, 7X
Flies	sizes 18 to 6

TROUT: Light, spring creeks

Rod	7 to 9 feet, 1 to 4 weight, slow to medium action
Reel	Lightweight click-drag single action. Capacity: Up to DT 4F and 50 yards of backing
Backing	50 yards of 20-pound braided Dacron
Fly lines	Matched to rod (1, 2, 3, or 4) 1. Double-taper floating 2. Weight-forward floating
Leader	10-, 12-, or 16-foot knotless spring creek or midge-nymph taper with 4X, 5X, 6X, or 7X tip
Tippets	4X, 5X, 6X, 7X, 8X
Flies	sizes 28 to 14

TROUT: Medium, small to medium-sized streams, beaver ponds, and small lakes

Rod	8$\frac{1}{2}$ to 9 feet, 4, 5, or 6 weight, medium to medium-fast action
Reel	Single action, with click or disc drag. Capacity: Up to WF 6F and 100 yards of backing
Backing	100 yards of 20-pound braided Dacron
Fly lines	Matched to rod (4, 5, or 6) 1. Weight-forward floating 2. Weight-forward sinking-tip
Leaders	Floating line: 9- to 12-foot all-purpose knotless taper Sinking line: 6-foot knotless sinking-line taper with 2X tip
Tippets	1X, 2X, 3X, 4X, 5X, 6X
Flies	sizes 18 to 4

TROUT and STEELHEAD: *Heavy, for medium and large rivers, large ponds, and lakes*

Rod	9 to 9¹/₂ feet, 7, 8, or 9 weight, medium-fast action with short extension butt on handle
Reel	Single action with disc drag. Capacity: Up to WF 9F and up to 150 yards backing. Extra spools
Backing	100 to 150 yards of 20-pound braided Dacron
Fly lines	Matched to rod (7, 8, or 9) 1. Weight-forward floating 2. Weight-forward sinking-tip 3. Weight-forward full-sinking
Leaders	Floating line: 9-foot knotless taper with 0X tip Sinking lines: 6-foot knotless sinking-tip taper, 0X-2X tip
Tippets	0X, 1X, 2X, 3X
Flies	sizes 6 to 2/0

PANFISH: *Medium, streams, ponds, rivers, and lakes*

Rod	7¹/₂ to 8¹/₂ feet, 4, 5, or 6 weight, medium action
Reel	Single action with click drag and extra spool. Capacity: Up to WF 6F and 50 feet of backing
Backing	50 feet of 20-pound braided Dacron
Fly lines	Matched to rod (4, 5, or 6) 1. Double-taper floating 2. Weight-forward floating 3. Weight-forward sinking-tip
Leaders	Floating lines: 7¹/₂- or 9-foot all-purpose knotless taper with 3X tip Sinking line: 6-foot knotless sinking-line taper with 3X tip
Tippets	3X, 4X, 5X
Flies	sizes 14 to 6

BASS: *Light to medium, streams, ponds, and lakes*

Rod	8¹/₂ to 9 feet, 6 or 7 weight, medium-fast action
Reel	Single action or multiplier with click drag. Capacity: Up to WF 7F and 100 yards of backing. Extra spools
Backing	50 to 100 yards of 30-pound braided Dacron
Fly lines	Matched to rod (6 or 7) 1. Weight-forward floating bass-bug taper 2. Weight-forward sinking-tip
Leaders	Floating lines: 9¹/₂-foot medium bass knotless taper with 1X tip Sinking line: 6-foot knotless sinking-line taper with 1X tip
Tippets	1X, 2X, 3X, 4X
Flies	sizes 10 to 2

BASS: Heavy, large rivers, lakes, swamps, canals, bayous

Rod	9 or $9^1/_2$ feet, 8, 9, or 10 weight, fast-action with a powerful, stiff butt
Reel	Large single action or multiplier with click drag. Capacity: Up to WF 10F and 150 yards of backing. Extra spools
Backing	100 to 150 yards of 30-pound braided Dacron
Fly lines	Matched to rod (8, 9, or 10) 1. Weight-forward floating bass-bug taper 2. Weight-forward sinking-tip 3. Weight-forward full-sinking
Leaders	Floating line: $9^1/_2$-foot heavy bass knotless taper with 0/2X to 0X tip Sinking line: 6-foot knotless sinking-line taper with 0/2X or 0X tip
Tippet	0/2X, 0/1X, 0X, 1X, and 2X
Flies	Sizes 4 to 5/0

SALMON: Heavy Atlantic salmon and Pacific salmon from 8 to 25 pounds

Rod	9, $9^1/_2$, or 10 feet, 8, 9, or 10 weight, medium-fast action with short extension butt on handle
Reel	Quality single action with disc drag. Capacity: Up to WF 10F and 250 yards of backing
Backing	150 to 250 yards of 30-pound braided Dacron
Fly lines	Matched to rod (8, 9, or 10) 1. Double-tapered floating 2. Weight-forward long-belly floating 3. Weight-forward sinking-tip 4. Uniform-sink 5. Shooting head
Leaders	Floating lines: 9-foot all-purpose knotless taper with 2X to 0X tip. Shooting head–sinking lines: 6-foot knotless sinking-line taper with 2X to 0X tip
Tippets	0X, 1X, and 2X
Flies	sizes 8 to 1/0

PIKE AND MUSKIE: *Heavy, lakes and large rivers*

Rod	9¹/₂ to 10 feet, 9, 10, 11, or 12 weight, fast action with stiff butt and extension butt on handle
Reel	Large single action with disc drag; two extra spools recommended. Capacity: Up to WF 12F and 200 yards of backing
Backing	150 to 200 yards of 30-pound braided Dacron
Fly lines	Matched to rod (9, 10, 11, or 12) 1. Weight-forward floating, saltwater, bass, or pike tapers 2. Weight-forward sinking-tip 3. Weight-forward uniform full-sinking
Leaders	Floating line: 9-foot heavy-butt bass, knotless tapered leader with 0/4X to 0X tip Sinking-tip and full-sinking lines: 6-foot knotless sinking-line taper with 0/4X to 0X tip
Tippets	0/5X, 0/4X, 0/2X, 0X
Bite Tippet	12-inch bite or shock tippet of stiff hard nylon in 40–80 pound test, or plastic-coated braided wire in 15–50 pound test
Flies	sizes 1/0 to 6/0, 3–8 inches long

GENERAL SALTWATER: *Coastal tidal rivers, bays, and surf for striped bass, bluefish, drum, and channel bass*

Rod	9 to 10 feet, 9 or 10 weight, fast action with powerful butt section; special saltwater models with extension butt
Reel	Large single action saltwater resistant with disc drag. Capacity: Up to WF 10F and 200 yards of backing
Fly lines	Matched to rod (9 or 10) 1. Weight-forward floating saltwater taper 2. Weight-forward sinking-tip 3. Sinking shooting-head system, sink rates of I, II, III, IV, V line densities
Leaders	Floating line: 9-foot knotless saltwater taper with 0/4X to 0X tip Sinking lines: 6-foot knotless sinking-line taper with 0/4X to 0X tip
Tippets	Fluorocarbon tippet, 12- to 20-pound test
Bite tippet (for bluefish)	12 inches of 15- to 30-pound wire attached to leader tip
Flies	sizes 6 to 3/0

BONEFISH: Medium to heavy; also good for other shallow-water casting to 2- to 15-pound saltwater fish such as redfish, sea trout (spotted weakfish), bonito, permit, snook, snapper, and ladyfish

Rod	9 feet, 7, 8, or 9 weight, medium-fast action with small extension butt on handle
Reel	Single action, smooth disc drag, saltwater resistant. Capacity: Up to WF 9F and 200 yards of backing
Backing	150 to 200 yards of 20-pound braided Dacron
Fly lines	Matched to rod (7, 8, or 9) 1. Weight-forward floating long-belly, special bonefish taper 2. Weight-forward intermediate monocore bonefish taper 3. Weight-forward sinking-tip
Leaders	Floating and intermediate lines: 9- to 12-foot knotless nylon or knotted fluorocarbon saltwater taper with 2X, 1X, or 0X tip Sinking-tip: 6-foot knotless sinking-line taper with 0X, 1X, or 2X tip.

NOTE: Bite tippet is not usually needed for bonefish and the other species listed. However, other fish such as shark, barracuda, snook, and tarpon may sometimes take bonefish flies and bite through the leader. Sharp coral heads and branches can also shear the tippet. This outfit can be easily used to fish for these additional abrasive-mouthed species by using a bite tippet of hard nylon or wire.

LARGE TARPON and SNOOK: Heavy, from 30 to 100 pounds plus

Rod	9 or 9^1/$_2$ feet, 10, 11, or 12 weight, extra-fast action with extra-stiff butt and extension butt on handle
Reel	Large single action saltwater resistant with strong, smooth disc-drag system. Capacity: Up to WF 12F and 250 yards of backing
Backing	200 to 250 yards of 30-pound braided Dacron
Fly lines	Matched to rod (10, 11, or 12) 1. Weight-forward floating saltwater or tarpon taper 2. Weight-forward intermediate 3. Weight-forward intermediate monocore tarpon taper 4. Weight-forward sinking-tip
Leader	9- to 12-foot saltwater taper with special 100 percent knot tip section design; 12- to 20-pound test class tippet
Bite Tippet	12 inches of hard Mason nylon in 40- to 100-pound test

TYING FLIES

Fly tying, the hand manufacture of fish food imitations for fly fishing, is a major facet of the sport. I consider it to be the *other half* of fly fishing. Anyone who can fly fish can— and I believe would really enjoy—learn to tie flies.

▼

Tying flies is an utterly fascinating and relaxing pastime that may very well double your pleasure and success at the sport of fly fishing. It is a perfect off-season indoor complement to fly fishing, and can provide just-the-right flies during fishing season. Imitating natural fish foods or creating attractor flies, then catching fish on your own handmade flies, is a unique pleasure, and it gives a great sense of pride. There is no limit to the fish foods you can imitate by tying flies.

Fly tying is merely wrapping a thread around a hook shank, binding to the hook various tying materials (hair, feathers, rubber, yarns, wools, plastics, and tinsel, to name a few) to simulate a fish food. With a basic set of simple tools, tying materials, and a few tying instructions, you can learn how to tie flies in a few hours. You will be amazed at how well fish will strike your own hand-tied flies. Over the ten years that I taught and managed the fly-fishing schools for L.L. Bean, three-quarters of our students caught fish on the first fly they tied.

Getting started fly tying is not expensive if you keep your involvement simple and basic, gradually expanding as your interest, skill, and finances allow. Since the cost of most commercial flies reflects the hand labor more than the materials, tying your own may cost you only a few cents each. Almost without exception, amateur fly tyers produce more flies than they can use, so the excess make wonderful gifts or create extra income to cover the expense of the sport.

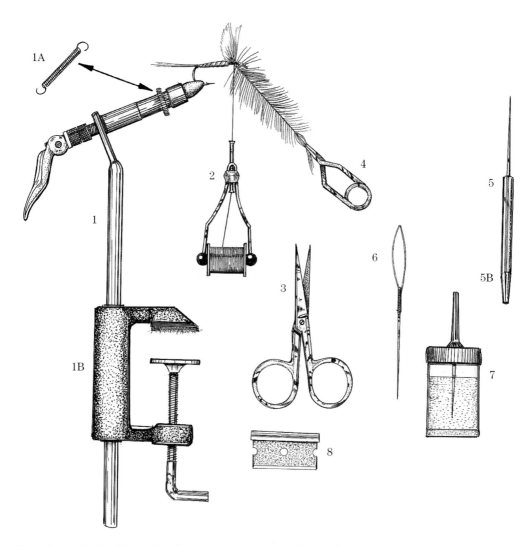

The Basic Fly-Tying Tools (approximate cost: $50 to $100)

1.   Vise: holds hook during tying

1A. Spring material clip: fits on the vise cam and holds materials ready for use

1B. Vise clamp attaches vise to table or desktops

2.   Bobbin: holds thread during tying

3.   Needle-point scissors: cuts and trims tying materials

4.   Hackle pliers: holds small or delicate feathers

5.   Bodkin and half-hitch tool: Bodkin point (5A) picks and separates materials
     Half-hitch tool (5B) helps form a the half-hitch knot

6.   Simple nylon-loop whip-finish tool: helps form whip-finish knot

7.   Fly-tying cement with applicator top: glues, coats, and adds finish

8.   Single-edge razorblade for cutting or trimming thread and materials

FLY-TYING MATERIALS

Natural materials, such as domestic and wild bird feathers, wild animal hair, and metallic tinsel, have been the traditional pillars of fly tying. In recent decades, however, fly tyers have come to accept a much greater range of materials, such as man-made synthetics, certain plant parts, and pen-raised domesticated birds and animals. There is ever-growing evidence that both hybrid natural materials and synthetic materials, if properly selected for texture, color, and size, perform equally well as or can even surpass the traditional natural materials for making quality, functional flies. Remember that most traditional and modern fly designs and their color patterns are simply products of fly tyers choosing from among the suitable materials that are locally available to them. There is practically no limit to the materials that can be used.

Tying tools, materials, hooks, instruction books, and videos are readily available from retail stores and catalogs. Helpful fly-tying classes may be found at local tying clinics, community colleges, fly-tying clubs, and sporting-goods stores. As you become more familiar with the tools and materials of fly tying, you will most likely enjoy making certain tools and gathering materials from hunting trips or excursions to garage sales, taxidermists, or sewing and craft-material stores. Discovering a new tool or material is a bonus adventure to the sport.

FLY-TYING HOOKS

Hooks are the foundation of all flies. They are available to accommodate almost any conceivable size, design, and imitation need of fly tyers. It is important to use the right hook for a fly's size, density, and intended performance.

Hook Parts

Eye The looped opening at the end of the hook to which the leader's tip or tippet is attached. Types of hook eyes include the straight, ringed eye (R), turned-up eye (TU), turned-down eye (TD), ball-eye (B), and looped eye (L). Try to select hooks with eyes that are completely closed.

Shank The hook's section between the eye and the bend that provides the length and foundation for attaching the materials. Shank lengths vary from extra short (XS) to extra long (XL).

Bend The curved portion that determines the hook shape. Some examples are round, limerick, and sproat bends.

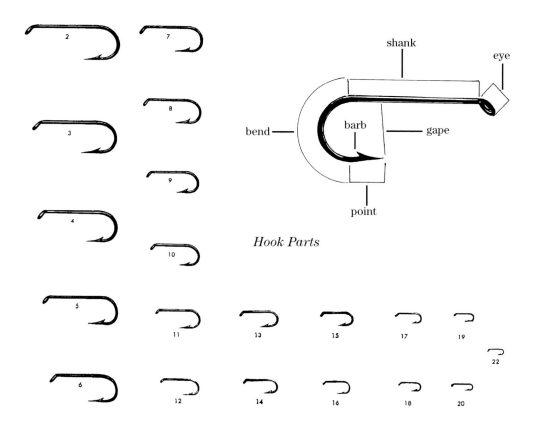

Hook Parts

Mustad #7958, actual size #2 to #22

Point The sharp or spear-shaped lower end portion that penetrates the fish's mouth. Chemically sharpened points are usually superior in sharpness.

Barb Just behind the point, the barb is designed to aid in keeping the hook lodged at the mouth tissue of the fish. Barbless hooks or those with microbarbs are best for fly fishing, since they allow fish to be released more easily.

Gap The vertical distance between the point and the shank.

TYING A WOOLLY WORM WET FLY

The Woolly Worm wet fly is a simple fly to tie, yet it involves many of the basic fly-tying procedures. It is also a very effective fly design for taking almost all types of fish. Listed on page 153 are the materials you will need to create your own Woolly Worm.

The versatile Woolly Worm in various color combos and sizes.

Hook:	Tiemco 5263 or Mustad 9672; TDE 2XL, size 6
Thread:	Waxed monocord, black or yellow
Tail:	Tip of hackle (rooster feather)
Body:	Medium black chenille
Body Hackle:	3- to 4-inch-long neck or saddle hackle
Cement:	Clear fly-tying cement (Dave's Flexament is recommended)

TYING PROCEDURE

Before you begin tying your first fly, carefully read over these instructions and study each illustration. Next, lay out all your tools and materials and seat yourself comfortably so that you can reach your vise and view it from the side and top. Make sure that you have a good light source angling from above and behind you toward the vise and table.

As you begin to tie the Woolly Worm or any other fly, strive to get the *proportions* correct. Use the hook to judge these, and study a sample fly or illustrations. If the proportions are correct, the fly will cast, swim, and hook properly.

Step 1A. Position the hook in the vise jaws so that the point and barb are not covered by the vise jaws and the shank is almost parallel to the tabletop. Tighten the jaws just enough to grip the hook firmly.

Step 1B. Pull out about 3 inches of thread from the bobbin. Hold it tight against the middle shank with your left hand; hold the bobbin in your right hand. Now wrap the thread firmly with the bobbin (held in your right hand) over, down, under, and back over the hook (clockwise) shank, working toward the hook eye. Stop just short of the eye, and wrap back over the first wraps. This

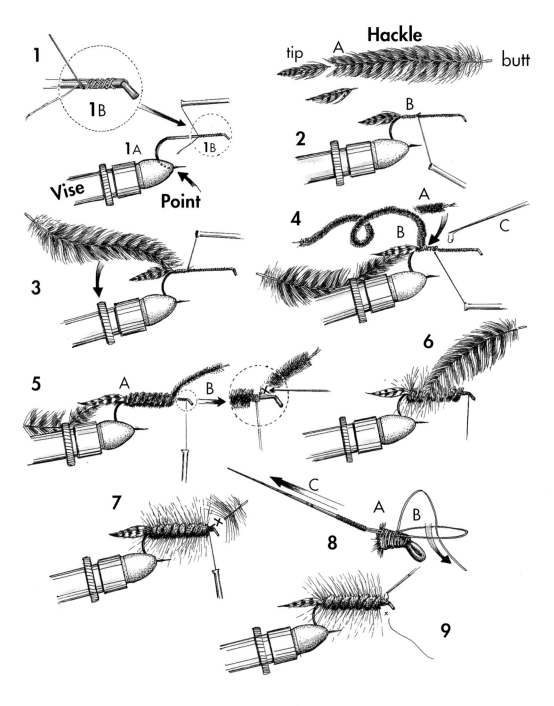

Steps for tying a Woolly Worm

jam-knot locks the thread on the hook shank. Now wrap the thread back to the hook bend and carefully trim away the excess thread tip with scissors. A thread-wrapped hook shank provides a better surface to attach and cement materials.

Step 2A. The tail. With your scissors, cut the tip off the end of the hackle feather for the fly's tail. It should be *one-third* as long as the hook shank.

Step 2B. With your left thumb and index finger, hold the hackle tip just over the junction of the hook shank and bend. With your thread bobbin, make about two or three loose wraps around the hook and the feather stem while still holding the feather tip exactly where you want it to be tied. Now tighten those wraps and make about six more over the hook and feather stem.

In most cases when attaching material to the hook shank with thread, making a few loose wraps first *and then* tightening will ensure that the material remains in position when the thread is tightened.

Release your hold on the feather, and check its position. If it seems a bit out of line, simply pull or twist it into position.

Step 3. Attaching hackle. Just at the end of the hook shank, next to the tail, place the hackle tip end with your left thumb and index finger. Wrap thread closely around it three or four times, and then tighten the wraps. Now make about six more tight wraps over the tied-down hackle end to secure it. Place the hackle butt in the materials clip.

Step 4A. Attaching body chenille. Cut a strand of chenille about four or five times the length of the hook shank. On one end, pull away some of the fuzzy fibers to expose about $1/8$ inch or more of the chenille's thread core.

Step 4B. Now place this chenille thread tip just beside the tail and hackle tie-down area (at the shank and bend junction) and wrap it down.

Step 4C. Body cementing. Lightly overcoat the entire hook shank with fly-tying cement. This glues the attached materials and seals the hook shank and thread wraps against water damage. It also provides additional adhesion for the body material that is next to be wrapped over the shank.

Step 5A. Body. *Important:* Advance the thread now to just behind the hook eye.

Step 5B. Wrap the chenille around the hook shank. Begin at the hook bend. Using a right-to-left-hand exchange, wrap the chenille in the same direction that the thread is wrapped. Space the wraps so that they just touch each other.

Step 5C. *Important:* Stop wrapping just before you get to the hook eye—about one hook-eye length away. Wrap thread across the chenille to tie it down to the hook shank. Make about six to eight firm thread wraps, and clip away the excess chenille with the tips of your scissors, *taking care not to cut the tying thread.*

Step 6. Body hackle. Grasp the hackle butt with your right hand and wrap the feather around the body from the hook bend to just behind the hook eye. Make a forward spiral wrap of between three and five turns. Try to position the wraps between the chenille wraps.

Step 7. When the hackle has been wrapped to behind the hook eye, make one full wrap around the shank and then tie down the stem with your thread. Carefully trim away the excess stem and butt with your scissor tips.

Do not crowd the hook eye with the hackle wrap or there will not be enough space to make the fly head and finish knot. Study the illustrations closely to avoid this and other possible problems with proportions and shaping.

Step 8A. With tying thread, wrap over the chenille and hackle tie-down area to cover them and to form a neat, small thread head. The head wraps should be just up to the hook eye but not over it. Make sure the wraps are smoothly placed and tight.

Step 8B. Head whip-finish. Place the whip-finish tool's nylon loop over the fly's head. Make about six to ten firm (but *not tight*) wraps over the loop and head, advancing from the back of the head toward the hook eye and loop end.

Step 8C. Pull about 6 inches of thread off the bobbin spool. While holding the thread tight with your left-hand fingers, cut the thread so it is about 3 or 4 inches long. Now place the cut thread end through the nylon loop. Keep tension on the thread so the wraps will not loosen or unwind.

Step 8D. Grasp the whip-finisher handle, keeping the loop *above* the hook eye, and pull back so that the loop slides under the wraps until it pulls free, pulling the thread end with it. Next, tighten the thread wraps of the whip-finish by pulling on the thread end. Trim away the excess thread with scissors as close as possible to the head.

Step 9. Head finish. Paint the thread wraps carefully with one or two coats of fly-tying cement. Take care not to plug the hook's eye with cement or allow any to get on the body or hackle. If this happens, blot the excess out of the hook eye before it can harden. A small feather or toothpick works nicely for this cleaning.

* * *

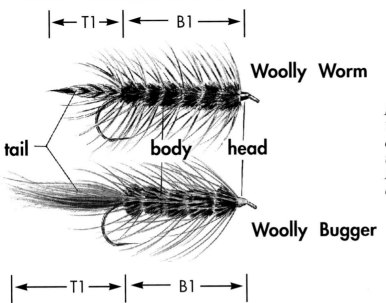

Woolly Worm

tail   body   head

Woolly Bugger

Porportions for the Woolly Worm and the Woolly Bugger: a Woolly Worm's tail is half the length of its body; a Woolly Bugger's tail is the same length as its body.

You have just accomplished many of the most important techniques and steps in fly tying. Repeat tying this fly several times at least, allowing time to relax and let your skill and dexterity develop. Each time, the tying will become more fun and you'll do much better, too.

By simply substituting a marabou feather tip for the hackle tip you can make a second important fly, the Woolly Bugger. Make the marabou tip tail equal to the hook-shank length. You can also vary the fly's size and the colors of chenille, hackle, or marabou to create a wide selection of effective Woolly Buggers and Woolly Worms.

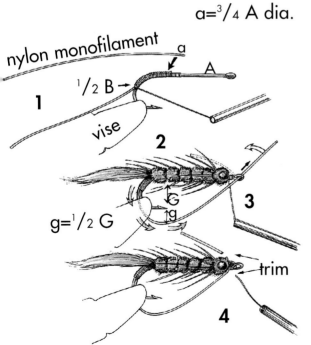

$a = {}^3/_4$ A dia.

Snag Guards

Most flies can be tied with a simple, flexible nylon monofilament loop to prevent many of the hang-ups on water structures.

1. *Attach a mono strand that is 3/4 the diameter of the hook wire (A) to the rear portion of the hook shank and half of the upper bend (B).*

2. *Tie the fly as you normally would.*

3. *Bend nylon strand down under hook and pass it through the underside of the hook eye. Loop formed (g) should extend half of the hook gap (G) below the hook point.*

4. *Using tying thread, wrap the nylon strand to bottom of hook behind the eye, then bend the upper part of the strand down and wrap it to upper hook shank behind the hook eye. Whip-finish, trim the excess strand away, and cut away thread. Coat the wraps with fly head cement.*

FLY-FISHING SAFETY

Fly fishing is an outdoor sport that requires attention to safety to avoid accidents. In addition to the constant threat of sunburn, the most common accidents experienced while fly fishing are falling, hooking yourself or another person, and being bitten or cut on hands or fingers by a fish. All are easily avoided or made less likely when you take a few basic precautions.

▼

AVOIDING FALLING

Most falls occur while you are approaching or leaving the water or while wading fast-flowing, irregular-bottomed streams. Loss of balance happens most frequently when you are in water from an inch deep to just above your knees. In such shallow water you have lots of confidence, and you tend to step or walk quickly and without caution. In deeper water you step more slowly and cautiously, and the deeper water helps hold you erect.

To avoid falls, be sure to wear a wading boot or shoe with a sole and heel made to grip the type of bottom you're on. Rubber-cleat soles are best for soft bottoms—sand, fine gravel, silt, or mud. Felt soles are best for hard bottoms made up of large, irregular-sized rocks and flat bedrock covered by slick algae. The felt actually scrubs the algae away and grips the rough rock surface. Take great care in walking up or down wet dirt, clay, or leaf-laden banks while wearing felt-soled shoes, however. These surfaces may be as slippery as ice against the wet, smooth felt.

In swift water over hard, slick rock bottoms, use soles that have felt and soft-metal stud or cleat combinations. The metal cuts slightly into the rock's surface. Take care with this combination while walking over dry rocks, as you lose some traction.

No sole material can compensate for careless footwork while wading. Learn to slowly shuffle and feel your footing from step to step. Do not pick up one foot until the other is firmly in place. Whenever possible, watch for bottom pitfalls using polarized sunglasses. Large boulders, flat, slick rocks, depressions, tree limbs, roots, mucky bottoms, loose rocks, and drop-offs can put you down quickly if you do not see, feel, or suspect them.

You will have an easier time wading if you use a wading staff as your searching "foot" or foundation as you take each step. You can select a stout streamside stick or buy a special wading staff. I recommend the Folstaff, which folds conveniently when not in use and immediately unfolds and automatically stiffens when you need it for wading or hiking to or from the stream.

Wade Carefully!

Try not to wade against the current. Wherever possible, cross by going with the current. If you begin to lose your footing or balance, you can slap your fly rod down on the water to regain balance without harming the fly rod. If you do fall or wade over your head, do not fight the current. Relax and go with it. Keep your feet downstream and your head upstream until the water or a friend helps you to safety. If you are fly fishing with a companion, help each other wade safely across bad stretches. One way is to place your hand on the other's shoulder or lock arms. Another way is to hold hands. Four legs are twice as safe as two—any dog, cat, or horse can tell you that!

Hip Boots

Hip boots are one of the most convenient ways to wade water, but they can also be the most dangerous if you fall or step into swift or deep water. Never wade in above your knees while wearing hip-high waders. Do not wear them in a boat or where you might step or fall into water over your head. Hip boots quickly fill and handicap your ability to swim.

Chest-High Waders

When wearing chest-high waders, *always* wear a belt snugly around their outside to prevent them from filling with water if you wade too deep or fall. It is a good idea to experiment by going too deep in waders or hippers in a swimming pool, with a friend standing by, just to get a sense of what would happen should you fall down or go too deep while fishing. The experience may well save your or another's life. Your clothing and waders will hold air and remain buoyant to a certain extent. This will keep you floating if you do not struggle or swim violently with your legs. Use your arms and fly rod to keep upright, and for swimming.

FISH BITES

Bites, cuts, or punctures from fish's sharp teeth, sharp gill-plate edges, and spined fins are common hand injuries. Some of these wounds are very painful, and occasionally infectious and even poisonous. So it pays to use certain precautions when landing and handling any fish. A dip net, a tailer, a gaff, and various mouth-opening and hook-removal tools will, if used properly, almost entirely eliminate these dangers. Protective gloves are also useful for handling and unhooking some fish, as well as when dressing a fish to eat.

First, do not get so excited when you land or unhook a fish that you forget to keep your hands and fingers away from its mouth, gill plates, and fins. Learn which fish can hurt, and how. For instance, all trout, char, and salmon have sharp teeth, but none have cutting gill plates or sharp, spined fins. A snook has a harmless mouth but razor-sharp gill plates and needle-sharp dorsal-fin spines.

So keep the fish out of your hands by using a net or by beaching it. Keep your fingers out of its mouth or off gill plates by using a hemostat, needle-nose pliers, or a hook disgorger to unhook it.

HOOKING ACCIDENTS

When you practice fly casting on the lawn or over water, use a hookless practice fly or cut the hook off an ordinary fly. Wear a brimmed or billed hat, glasses, a tight-weave long-sleeved shirt, and long trousers for protection. Such apparel almost completely protects you from the most common hooking accidents.

Watch where you and everyone else are located, and do not get in each other's casting paths. On windy days, be particularly careful about where your fly goes on the backcast. When your fly strikes and holds to an unseen object behind you, do not attempt to free it with more pulls until you know what it has caught on. It might be another person, your pet, or even yourself. Also, never try to jerk a hooked fly loose from hangups on backward or forward casts without taking care that it will not snap back and hit you.

When you wade, keep a good distance away from other anglers and watch the wind's effect on the fly. In a boat, be very careful of the other occupants, and try to keep the boat angled so you do not allow your backcast to travel over the boat. If you are right-handed and you cast from the bow to the shoreline, keep

How to remove a hook that has penetrated into the skin beyond the barb:

1. *Cut the leader.*

2. *Place a loop of monofilament around the hook bend and press the fly head down.*

3. *Press down on the leader directly before the fly and make a quick, straight pull back with the loop.*

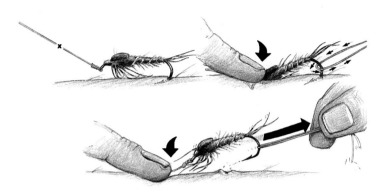

the boat moving parallel to the *left* shoreline. Then your backcast will be ahead of the boat. The opposite is best for the left-handed caster.

If you should hook yourself or someone else, there are several actions you might take for safe hook removal. First, it is essential to relax the hooked person with assurances, then remove the hook as promptly and painlessly as possible (or get to an emergency room quickly) in order to avoid the person going into shock.

If it is a barbless hook, just grasp the fly and remove it by reversing the entry path. If the hook has a barb and it has penetrated past the barb, the situation may be a bit more serious. First, do not panic. After all, the hook has done very little tissue damage, so just relax. Ninety-nine percent of all hooks can be painlessly and quickly removed.

If you have hooked yourself and someone is with you, let your companion remove the hook; if you are alone, you can remove the hook if you can easily reach it with both hands. If you cannot, cut the leader tip off the fly and seek help elsewhere.

Should the fly be lodged in the eye socket area, or buried in the skull bones or in the throat or neck, *go immediately to the emergency room of the nearest hospital!*

Here are steps to follow when the situation is one in which you decide that you or a companion should remove the hook: (1) Cut off the leader at or near the fly eye, and put your fly rod aside. (2) Determine if the hook is just buried or has turned and exited the skin. Most hooks will be buried. If it is only buried to or just past the bend, follow Procedure A. Follow Procedure B if it is turned back out.

Hook Removal: Procedure A (for a hook buried to or just past the bend): Take a section of heavy nylon monofilament, or other fishing line or fly line, long enough to secure a firm handhold on when it is doubled. Pass it through the hook bend and back toward the direction opposite where the hook entered. With one hand, take a firm grip on the doubled section of line, just a few inches from the hook bend. With the other hand, press down the hook eye (fly-head area) with your index finger or thumb against the skin. While pressing down on the hook eye, make a straight, smooth, quick, firm pull on the doubled line *away from or opposite the direction the hook entered.* The fly will pop out immediately without much pain or tissue damage. Some bleeding may occur, but that is okay as it will help flush the wound. Encourage the bleeding a while, then stop it by applying direct pressure.

Hook Removal: Procedure B (for a hook that is turned back out): This removal method can only be attempted if you have a pair of side-cutting diagonals (dikes) or pliers. If you do not, do not attempt removal but go to a hospital emergency room or to a physician for assistance. Check the hook to see if the barb has cleared the skin. If it has not, push it on out with the pliers. Cut off the point and barb with side-cutting pliers and remove the debarbed hook by backing it out along the same path by which it entered. Allow the wound to bleed, then stop it with direct pressure.

In either case, treat the wound with antiseptic and cover it temporarily with a sterile bandage. As soon as convenient, consult a physician about the need for a tetanus shot.

My golden rule is never to fly fish with a barbed hook or with a companion or student who doesn't have on a barbless fly. If all fly fishers would observe this, being hooked would seldom be painful or dangerous.

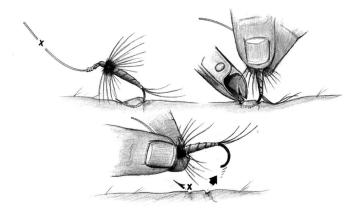

How to remove the hook when the point has penetrated skin and emerged:

1. *Cut the leader.*
2. *Rotate and push hook point up until barb emerges. Cut off point and barb.*
3. *Back hook out of entrance.*

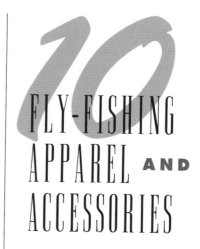

FLY-FISHING APPAREL AND ACCESSORIES

Fly fishing, being an on-the-water, all-season outdoor sport, requires certain apparel and accessories to provide comfort, efficiency, and safety.

▼

Clothing   No matter what season or weather you fly fish in, you will function best if your clothes are as light as conditions allow: loose, comfortable, breathable, and nonbinding. They should be functional, not impractically stylish or fancy. Choose layered clothes that breathe and give you protection against sun, wind, dampness, and insects. For practicality, avoid nonwashable fabrics. To avoid being seen by fish and biting insects, choose subtle, natural colors.

Fishing hats   The ideal hat for fly fishing should have a good visor and brim to give your head and neck protection from sun, glare, wind, and insects. It should be reasonably rainproof and fit snugly enough so that the wind will not blow it off; a chin or safety strap is handy in high winds. Under certain conditions, you may want a hat that will accommodate a bug net. A fringe benefit of wearing a hat is that it protects you from getting hooked in the head.

Rain and wind jackets   A good jacket must be rainproof. The most practical jacket for wading folds into a small bundle and fits inside your fishing-vest back pocket or your wader pouch. For wading, it should not go below your waist. It should have a hood that will comfortably fit over your head and hat. Drawstrings at the hood and waist and snug wristbands help keep out rain, insects, and wind. Be sure your jacket will fit over your normal outerwear, including fishing vest. Do not waste your money on jackets that are made from plastic that hardens or stiffens in cold weather.

If you intend to fish without waders from shore or from a boat, your jacket should extend at least below your hips for ample protection.

Fishing vests and chest packs   For fly fishing on foot, a fishing vest or chest pack is extremely useful. It should contain enough well-designed pockets to carry what you will need for an entire day's fishing. This includes fly boxes, rain jacket, sunglasses, film, and so on. Choose a lightweight model without too many pockets. Shorty-style vests are most practical for the fly fisher who wades fairly deep. If you are a nonswimmer or you regularly wade treacherous deep water, a flotation fishing vest is strongly recommended. I prefer a model with built-in flotation over the gas inflatables. When fishing from shore or a boat, you may choose to use a tackle box or kit tackle bag instead of a vest or chest pack.

Chest packs are an increasingly popular alternative for carrying fly boxes and small accessories. Access to these items is somewhat more convenient than with a vest, but some fly fishers find them a bit more bulky and in the way. I recommend that you try both and decide for yourself.

Waders   For cold-water wading, chest-high waders are a necessity. There are two designs: the stocking-foot wader and the boot-foot wader.

Stocking-foot waders are more portable and lightweight, and allow more freedom of movement. They are better for getting in and out of boats and floatplanes, for backpacking, and for float-tube fishing. You must wear thick socks or gravel guards and good, sturdy wading shoes over the feet of stocking-foot waders.

Boot-foot waders are generally more durable, heavier, and warmer but can restrict leg movement more. These waders are faster and easier to put on and take off, as the shoe or boot is part of them. When the fishing is easily accessible, boot-foot waders are a better overall choice for the fly fisher.

If you plan to fish in colder weather and wade deep, cold water, and you have no weight-load problems, then insulated waders are ideal, especially those made from neoprene. Insulated boot-foot waders are best for extreme cold. Lightweight waders are less durable but more portable and less tiring to wear. They are more practical in warmer conditions. In very cold conditions, extra underwear and stocking insulation can be worn.

For hot weather, cold-water wading, or tubing, choose lightweight stocking-foot waders. The breathable lightweight waders made from Gore-Tex or similar fabrics are ideal for avoiding excessive condensation inside your waders. It's important to avoid abrasive surfaces or kneeling with lightweight waders to prevent leaks. If Gore-Tex waders seem to seep water, usually washing them cleans the fabric so it can function correctly.

USEFUL FLY-FISHING ACCESSORIES

Polarized sunglasses— a must for fly fishing	Compass
	Band-aids
Wading staff	Matches (waterproof) or butane lighter
Creel	
Clippers	Small whistle
Hook sharpener	Folding cup
Scissors/pliers	Insect repellent
Leader wallet	Small knife
Fly boxes	Patch kit
Fly flotant	Lip balm
Fly-line dressing	Hemostat
Paper towels	Thermometer
Leader-tippet spools	Small aquarium net
High-energy bar	Sunblock
Ten-foot cord	Small bottle of water

For extremely warm conditions, you might want to just wade wet. Shorts or jeans, with good wading shoes and heavy socks, will work nicely. Long pants with polypropylene long underwear work nicely for cold-water wet-wading. Always wear long pants and high-top wading shoes with thick soles when wading saltwater flats, bars, and bays. This is important to avoid injuries resulting from encounters with barnacles, corals, stinging creatures, and other hazards.

Wader boots, like hiking boots, should give you protection against ankle, foot, and toe bruises and sprains. More importantly, they should give good bottom traction. There are three general types of boot soles:

Rubber cleats are best for soft mud, clay, and sand bottoms, but very dangerous on slick bedrock or rubble-rock bottoms.

Felt soles are good for hard bedrock and rubble-rock bottoms where there is moderately swift water or very slick algae. Felt soles are poor for mud, sand, or clay bottoms.

Soft-metal cleat or stud soles are ideal for hard bedrock or large-rubble bottoms that are very slick, or in very swift water. They are fair to good for soft-bottom wading. Metal cleats are impractical, however, for wearing in boats or rafts or on dry rock.

Felt or metal-cleat wading sandals, which fit over either wading shoes or the boots of waders, are very convenient when you want to convert quickly and simply from one sole to another.

Wader suspenders, belts, and patch kits are absolutely necessary accessories for waist- and chest-high waders.

Hip-high wading boots are a popular, convenient, comfortable means of fishing from shorelines and wading shallow water. Do not use them for boat wear or wading areas over your knees. If you go in too deep, they quickly fill with water and will disable your legs for swimming and balance.

Wader belts and wading staffs are two important safety items. The snug wader belt will take part of the wader weight off your shoulders, but more importantly, it will keep your waders from filling with water if you fall or go into water that's too deep. The wading staff can serve as a third leg while you wade slick or swift water, or assist in testing the depth ahead of you. It also helps you negotiate stream shorelines or steep trails.

11

THE PRESENT AND YEARS AHEAD: ETHICS AND MANNERS

Once you've learned the basics of fly fishing, you're ready to reap the rewards. You'll find that fly fishing will greatly multiply your pleasure on the water; you'll enjoy the process of casting itself, and you'll enjoy the special thrill of tempting a really difficult fish to your fly—perhaps one you've tied yourself.

▼

It won't all be easy. You can't learn all of fly fishing in a week or from any book. Skill takes motivation and regular practice. You'll have to be patient with your flaws and try steadily to correct them. There will be frustrations—wind knots, sloppy casts, the inability to match a specific hatch of insects when fish are rising to them everywhere in sight, times when you're fly tying and you seem to have nine thumbs. You must *want* to perfect your techniques and you must practice constantly. Believe me, it's worth the effort. This sport has given me over fifty years of pleasure.

Fly fishing can provide you a lifetime of pleasure, too—and part of that pleasure lies in improving your skills, becoming more adept at the various arts of fly fishing, and gaining more and more experience on the water.

Of course, the future of *your* fly fishing depends in part upon the future of everyone's fly fishing, and that depends upon the protection of our quarry and of the waters in which they live. More and more people are coming to love the *quality* of their fishing. They want to fish for wild fish in clean, natural surroundings. Fewer people are killing their fish today. They realize that tempting a fish to the fly and playing it on sensitive fly tackle is often the best part of fishing, and that releasing them provides fish to tempt another day. Sections of many rivers are now under "catch-and-release" restrictions, and the quality of the fishing they provide has improved immensely.

I began to fish actively at age six. My parents and grandparents were all anglers, and they were wonderful role models. They taught me not only how to catch fish, but also how to respect fish, other anglers, and the outdoors. The longer I live, the more I realize how fortunate I was to have such good early guidance. Today, many new anglers are entering the sport without parental role models or mentors, and must learn about outdoor behavior and respect from other anglers or teachers.

The first rule to follow is, as always, the Golden Rule: "Do unto others as you would have them do unto you." Be considerate, in other words, and try to avoid distracting or interfering with other anglers. Here is a list of good fishing manners:

- Do not crowd other anglers. Let them fish an entire pool if they get there first. Give them space.

- Do not rush ahead of another angler. Either fish a good distance behind or walk on shore past a long stretch of water past, at least into the next pool or bend in the river.

- If the water is already crowded, do not make matters worse by squeezing in, too.

- Ask other anglers in the area if you may share the water. If they say okay, do so carefully and don't get in their way, put down (scare) their fish, or make excessive conversation while they try to concentrate on their fishing.

- If you have a good spot and you notice other anglers waiting for a chance to fish it, either give up the spot after you have fished it a while or invite them to share the water with you.

- When you pass other anglers on foot, wading, or in a boat, make a circle around them as widely and quietly as it takes to not disturb them or the fish. Avoid loud greetings and remarks as others fish.

- If you are in a powerboat, be very careful not to throw a high wake when you are near bank anglers, waders, or people in small boats, tubes, or kickboats.

- Some public salmon rivers have rules about rotating through the pools, giving each angler a reasonable time to fish through. Follow this system strictly. This is an excellent way to share any trout or bass stream as well.

- Do not litter, especially with cigarette butts. They are offensive for others to see and harm fish and birds that eat them.

- When you hook or lose a fish, refrain from loud speech, profanity, screaming, or other noises that interfere with other anglers' serenity.

- When going to fish private land or water, ask permission first and take care where you park, walk, eat, clean fish, and toilet. Walk on paths; go under fences, or use styles or gates; always close gates; avoid frightening livestock; and do not litter.

- Pick up other people's litter (cans, strike indicators, cigarette butts, gum wrappers, and so on). Litter tends to attract more litter.

- Respect the rights of any legal angler. All sportfishing methods are just as worthy as fly fishing. Don't give other anglers a hard time if they choose other methods.

- Even if you release most fish you hook, don't become a numbers hog. Be conservative about how many fish you fight and handle on any given day. Catching alone puts a burden on the fish—and the fishery. I have a Texas friend, Paul, who after we catch eight or ten bass each will say, "Dave, I'm not mad at these bass, so let's stop and give them a break."

- Don't walk up to and peer over a high bank where others are fishing; your profile can put down rising fish and scare them away.

- As you travel to and from fishing waters and while you fish, endeavor to inflict as little foot damage as you can. Take care not to wade over fish nests, break down soft banks, or otherwise disturb the fishery. Never throw sticks or stones into a trout river.

One of the nicest common veins fly fishers seem to share is an unselfish attitude toward other fly fishers, especially those needing help with tackle, flies, casting, or techniques. I have always been proud of us for being that way. Be sure to take advantage of it now; and later, when you are thus skilled, help those who are as you were once yourself.

Because a lot of serious anglers have worked hard to protect our waters, the future of fly fishing is bright today. But you'll have to help if it's to remain so. Keep improving your skills; keep trying to catch more species of fish on the fly; help protect our fisheries—and have lots of fun fly fishing!

Appendix I
FLY ASSORTMENTS

STARTER TROUT ASSORTMENT

1. Parachute Adams, #14 (Dry Fly)
2. Royal Wulff, #10 (Dry Fly)
3. Elk-Hair Caddis, #12 (Dry Fly)

Elk-Hair Caddis dry fly—tan/olive

4. Dave's Hopper, #10 (Terrestrial)
5. Black Ant, #14 (Terrestrial)
6. Gold-Ribbed Hare's Ear, #14 (Nymph)
7. Red Fox Squirrel Nymph, #10 (Nymph)
8. Zug Bug, #12 (Nymph)
9. Muddler Minnow, #8 (Streamer)
10. Woolly Bugger, black and olive, #8 (Streamer)
11. Clouser Minnow, #6 (Streamer)

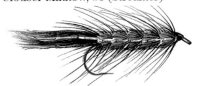

Woolly Bugger—Olive & Black Bugger

12. Near Nuff Sculpin, tan and olive, #8 (Streamer)

STARTER PANFISH ASSORTMENT

1. Sneaky Pete, black and chartreuse, #10
2. Sponge Spider, black and yellow, #10
3. Most Whit Hair Bug, yellow, #10
4. Humpy, orange belly, #12
5. Dave's Hopper, #8
6. Tellico Nymph, #12

7. Red Fox Squirrel Nymph, #10
8. Woolly Bugger, yellow or black, #8
9. Clouser Minnow, chartreuse and white, #8
10. Black Marabou Minijig, #10

STARTER BASS ASSORTMENT

1. Most Whit Hair Bug, Fruit Cocktail, #6
2. Near Nuff Frog, #10
3. Popper, yellow or black, #4
4. Pencil Popper, white and pearl, #4
5. Sheep Streamer, shad, #6
6. Lectric Leech, black, #4
7. Near Nuff Crayfish, brown, #6
8. Clouser Minnow, brown and white, #4
9. Woolly Bugger, olive or black, #4
10. Eelworm Streamer, purple or black, #2
11. Dahlberg Strip Diver, chartreuse or white, #2

Dahlberg Strip Diver—chartreuse

12. Frog Diver, orange belly, #6

STANDARD DRY-FLY SELECTION FOR TROUT

Adams, #14, #16, #18
Light Cahill, #12, #16, #18
Quill Gordon, #12, #14, #16
Black Gnat, #14, #16, #18
Blue-Winged Olive, #14, #16, #18

Appendix I: Fly Assortments

Hendrickson, #10, #12, #14
March Brown, #10, #12, #14

Special Dry Flies
Gray Fox Variant, #12, #14
Brown Spider, #10, #12
Dun Variant, #14, #16
Brown Bivisible, #10, #12
Parachute Adams, #12, #14, #16
Irresistible, #12, #14, #16
Royal Wulff, #10, #14
Henryville Caddis, #12, #14, #16

Dry-Fly Terrestrials
Black Ant, #12, #14, #16
Cinnamon Ant, #14, #16, #18
Beetle (black), #10, #14, #18
Dave's Hopper, #8, #10, #12
Jassid, #16, #18, #20
Green Inchworm, #10, #12, #14
Cricket (black), #10, #12, #14

Match-the-Hatch Dry-Fly Series
No-Hackles or Comparaduns
Dun, gray wing, yellow body, #16, #18, #20

*Comparadun
dry fly—Dorthea*

Slate gray wing, olive body, #14, #16, #18, #20
Slate gray wing, tan body, #12, #14, #18, #20
No-Hackle Hen or Poly Spinners
White wing, black body, #18, #20, #22
Light gray wing, yellow body, #16, #18, #20
Light gray wing, reddish brown body, #14,
   #16, #18
Light gray wing, gray-olive body, #12, #14, #16

Paraduns
Dun gray wing, tan body, #8, #10, #12
Slate gray wing, olive body, #8, #10, #12
Cream wing, yellow body, #6, #8, #10

Elk-Hair Caddis or Borger Poly Caddis (dry flies)
Tan wing, brown body, #12, #14, #16, #18
Tan wing, olive body, #14, #16, #18
Tan wing, gray body, #12, #14, #16
Tan wing, orange body, #6, #8, #10

STANDARD WET FLIES
Leadwing Coachman, #10, #12, #14
Royal Coachman, #10, #12, #14
Light Cahill, #12, #14
Parmachene Belle, #8, #10, #12
Black Gnat, #12, #14, #16
Iron Blue Dun, #12, #14, #16
Gray Hackle Yellow, #10, #12, #14
Gray Hackle Peacock, #10, #12, #14
Black and Grizzly Woolly Worm, #6, #8, #10

Nymphs
Gold-Ribbed Hare's Ear, #10, #12, #14, #16
Tellico, #10, #12
Zug Bug, #10, #12, #14
Darkstone, #2, #4, #6
Brownstone, #4, #6, #8
Goldenstone, #6, #8, #10
Dave's Shrimp, #12, #14, #16

Dave's Shrimp

Gray Nymph, #8, #10, #12
Red Squirrel Nymph, #8, #10, #12, #14
Damsel Nymph, #8, #10

STANDARD STREAMER ASSORTMENT
Clouser Minnow, #2, #6, #10
Near Nuff Sculpin, #6, #8, #10
Woolly Bugger, #6, #8, #10
Deep Sheep Streamer, #2, #4, #6
Gray Ghost, #2, #6, #10
Black-nose Dace, #4, #6, #8
Mickey Finn, #6, #8, #10
Muddler Minnow, #2, #6, #10
Black Ghost, #4, #6, #8
White Marabou, #2, #4, #6
Yellow Marabou, #6, #8, #10
Dark Spruce, golden, #2, #4, #6, #8
Light Spruce, silver, #4, #6, #8, #10
Hornberg, #2, #4

SALMON FLIES (WET)
Silver Gray, #2, #6, #8

Blue Charm, #2, #6, #8, #10
Rusty Rat, #4, #6, #8, #10
Black Dose, #4, #6, #8, #10
Cosseboom, #2, #4, #6, #8
Jock Scott, #2, #4, #6
Muddler, #2, #4, #6, #8
Butterfly, #4, #6, #8

SALMON FLIES (DRY)
Bomber, #1/0, #4, #8
White Wulff, #4, #6, #8
Rat-Faced McDougal, #4, #6, #8
Mackintosh, #2, #4, #6
Salmon Skater, #8
Dave's Adult Stonefly, #2, #4, #6

BASS- AND PIKE-BUG ASSORTMENT (TOP-WATER)
Dave's Diving Frog, yellow and orange belly,
    #2, #6
Dahlberg Strip Diver, chartreuse and black,
    #2, #4
Sneaky Pete, chartreuse and black, #2, #8
Umpqua Trophy Baitfish, red and yellow,
    yellow perch, #2, #2/0
Most Whit Hair Bug, yellow, black, red, and
    white, #2, #6, #10
Near Nuff Hair Frog, #2, #6, #10
Hula Popper, yellow, frog, black, #1/0, #4
Pencil Popper, yellow, white, black, #1/0, #4
Slider Bug, yellow, black, white, #1/0, #4
Sneaky Pete, chartreuse and black, #4, #8
Muddler Minnow, natural, black, white,
    yellow, #1/0, #4, #8
Dalberg Diver, frog, yellow, black, grizzly, sil-
    ver minnow, and perch, #2, #6, #10

FLATS ASSORTMENT (BONEFISH, REDFISH, PERMIT)
Chico's Bonefish Special, #4, #6, #8
Dave's Salt Shrimp, #4, #6, #8
Crazy Charlie, white, tan, #4, #6, #8
Clouser Minnow, chartreuse and white, #1/0,
    #4, #6

Snapping Shrimp, brown, #4, #6, #8
McCrab, tan or blue, #4, #1/0
Puff, tan or white, #4, #1/0
Swimming Crab, tan or brown, #2, #4, #6
Baited Breath, white, #6, #8, #10
Flats Popper, red and white, #4, #1/0
Horror, brown, #6, #8, #10

SALTWATER ASSORTMENT (TARPON, STRIPER, JACK, BARRACUDA, BLUEFISH, MACKEREL, DRUM, SNOOK)
Eelworm streamer, black, yellow, white,
    #1/0, #4
Grass Shrimp, gray, pink, tan, gold, #1/0, #4,
    #8, #10
Glass Minnow, white, blue and white, brown
    and white, #1/0, #4, #6, #8
Sea Ducer, red and yellow, red and white,
    #2/0, #4
Lefty's Deceiver, white, yellow, roach, red
    and white, black, blue and white, #2/0, #2,
    #6
Tarpon Special, yellow grizzly, blue grizzly,
    cockroach, orange grizzly, #3/0, #1/0
Skipping Popper, red and white, yellow, blue
    and white, #3/0, #1/0
Pencil Popper, yellow, white, silver, black,
    #3/0, #1/0, #4
Muddler Minnow, #3/0, #1/0, #4, #8

Dave's Hopper

Appendix II

PUBLICATIONS AND ORGANIZATIONS FOR FLY FISHERS

BOOKS ON FLY TYING

Most Important

Fly Tying Made Clear and Simple by Skip Morris
Flies (new edition) by J. Edson Leonard
Fly Tying Materials by Eric Leiser
Universal Fly Tying Guide by Dick Stewart (excellent for beginners)

Excellent

American Nymph Fly Tying Manual by Randall Kaufmann
Art of Tying the Dry Fly by Skip Morris (excellent for beginners)
Bass Flies by Dick Stewart
Designing Trout Flies by Gary Borger
The Fly Tyer's Almanac by Robert Boyle and Dave Whitlock
Popular Fly Patterns by Terry Hellekson
Salt Water Flies by Kenneth Bay
Tying the Swisher and Richards Flies by Doug Swisher and Carl Richards
Tying Bass and Panfish Flies by Skip Morris

Good

Atlantic Salmon Flies and Fishing by Joseph D. Bates Jr.

Bug Making by C. Boyd Pfeiffer
The Complete Book of Fly Tying by Eric Leiser
Dick Surette's Fly Index by Dick Surette
Dyeing and Bleaching Natural Fly-Tying Materials by A. K. Best
Flies for Alaska by Anthony Route
Salmon Flies by Poul Jorgensen
Streamers and Bucktails by Joseph D. Bates Jr.
Tying and Fishing Terrestrials by Gerald Almy
Western Trout Fly Tying Manual by Jack Dennis

BOOKS ON FLY FISHING

Most Important

Dave Whitlock's Guide to Aquatic Trout Foods by Dave Whitlock
Fishing the Flats by Mark Sosin and Lefty Kreh
Fly Fishing in Salt Water by Lefty Kreh
L.L. Bean Fly-Fishing for Bass Handbook by Dave Whitlock
Masters on the Dry Fly, edited by J. Migel
Masters on the Nymph, edited by J. Migel and Leonard Wright

Selective Trout by Doug Swisher and Carl
  Richards
Steelhead Fly Fishing by Trey Combs

Excellent
Bonefishing with a Fly by Randall
  Kaufmann
The Caddis and the Angler by Larry
  Solomon and Eric Leiser
Caddisflies by Gary LaFontaine
The Essence of Flycasting by Mel Kreiger
Fishing the Dry Fly as a Living Insect
  by Leonard Wright
Fly Casting with Lefty Kreh by Lefty Kreh
Fly Fishing for Trout by Dick Talleur
*Fly Fishing for Trout—Imitating and
  Fishing Natural Fish Foods* by Dave
  Whitlock
Fly Fishing Strategy by Doug Swisher and
  Carl Richards
Naturals by Gary Borger
Presentations by Gary Borger
Strategies for Stillwater by Dave Hughes
Through the Fish's Eye by Mark Sosin and
  John Clark

FLY-FISHING PERIODICALS

These magazines have up-to-date
features and advertisements to keep
you abreast of all you need to know
about fly fishing today.

The Flyfisher, P.O. Box 1595,
  Bozeman, MT 59771
  The official magazine of the Federation
  of Fly Fishers (FFF), published quarterly.
  Membership to FFF includes subscription
  to the magazine.
Flyfishing, P.O. Box 02112, Portland, OR
  97202
  Features fly fishing and fly tying.
Fly Fisherman, Box 8200, Harrisburg, PA
  17105
  Feature articles on fly fishing and fly
  tying throughout the world.
Fly Rod and Reel, P.O. Box 370, Camden,
  ME 04843
  Interesting fly-fishing articles.
The Roundtable, United Fly Tyers, Inc., P.O.
  Box 723, Boston, MA 02102

Membership in United Fly Tyers, a non-
profit international organization, includes
subscription. Articles on fly tying with
how-to instruction.
Salmon Trout Steelheader, P.O. Box 02112,
  Portland, OR 97202
  Often describes how to tie the best west-
  ern patterns.
Scientific Angler's Handbooks, Scientific
  Anglers, P.O. Box 2001, Midland, MI
  48640
  Annual handbooks on general fly fishing,
  bass fly fishing, panfish fly fishing, and
  saltwater fly fishing.
Trout, 1500 Wilson Boulevard, Arlington, VA
  22209
  The official magazine of Trout Unlimited
  (TU), published quarterly. TU member-
  ship includes subscription.
American Angler, P.O. Box 4100,
  Bennington, VT 05201-4100
Fly Fishing and Fly Tying, Game and Fish
  Publications, 8 The Square, Aberfetdy,
  Perthshire, PH 15 2DD
Fly Fishing in Salt Water, 2001 Western
  Avenue, Suite 210, Seattle, WA 98121
Fly Tackle Dealer, Roxmont, Route 1,
  Rockport, ME 04856
Infisherman, Infisherman Inc., Two In-
  Fisherman Drive, Brainerd, MN 56401-
  0999
The Nature Conservancy, 1815 North Lynn
  Street, Arlington, VA 22209
Saltwater Fly Fishing, P.O. Box 4100,
  Bennington, VT 05201-4100
Wild Steelhead and Salmon, 2315 210th
  Street, SE, Bothell, WA 98021-4206

MAJOR FLY-FISHING ORGANIZATIONS

Federation of Fly Fishers, P.O. Box 1595,
  Bozeman, MT 59771
  The federation has hundreds of clubs
  nationally and many internationally, con-
  ducting all types of fly-fishing, fly-tying,
  and conservation activities. With membership you receive an excellent news
  bulletin and *The Flyfisher* magazine.

Trout Unlimited, P.O. Box 1944, Washington,
  DC 20013

Trout Unlimited has chapters throughout the United States and Canada. It emphasizes trout and salmon fishing and conservation activities. Local chapters are active in fly-fishing and fly-tying seminars. With membership you receive a news bulletin and *Trout* magazine.

United Fly Tyers, Inc., P.O. Box 723, Boston, MA 02102

Active in all types of fly-tying and fly-fishing promotion and instruction. Has excellent magazine, *The Roundtable*, on fly tying.

Saltwater Fly Rodders Of America, P.O. Box 304, Cape May Court House, NJ 08120

Active in all types of saltwater fly fishing and fly tying. Also has magazine with membership.

The Nature Conservacy, 1815 North Lynn Street, Arlington, VA 22209

FLY-FISHING AND FLY-TYING VIDEOTAPES

Videotapes are excellent for home educational viewing and practicing.

The Essence of Flycasting by Mel Krieger. An excellent tape on learning Mel's flycasting methods.

The Skills of Fly Fishing by Gary Borger. Good introduction and teaching tape on fly fishing.

Anatomy of a Trout Stream by Rick Hafele. Excellent tape for learning about trout, how and where they live and feed.

Dave Whitlock's Fly Fishing for Bass. Excellent and exciting tape on how to fly fish for bass.

Strategies for Selective Trout by Doug Swisher. An excellent tape on how to read water and fish for trout more successfully.

Fly Fishing for Steelhead by Lani Waller. Good tape for the beginner steelhead fly fisher.

L.L. Bean Introduction to Fly Fishing with Dave Whitlock. An excellent companion tape to this handbook for beginners.

Bass Pro—Tying Bass Flies with Dave Whitlock. Dave ties his four favorite bass flies, the Most Whit Hair Bug, Frog Diver, Shad, and Harejig.

Fly Tying Basics with Jack Dennis. A good tape with which to learn to tie flies.

Most fly fishers discover that tying your own flies is easily as much fun and rewarding as fly fishing . . . I consider it to be the other half of fly fishing!

GLOSSARY

Action—A word that expresses the flexibility and power of a fly rod.

AFTMA—American Fishing Tackle Manufacturers Association. American fishing-tackle manufacturers organized to maintain standards of fishing tackle, public information, product quality, marketing, and conservation of the resource.

Arbor—The spindle of a fly-reel spool that the backing line is attached to and wound on.

Aquatic insects—Those insects that live some part of their normal life cycle beneath the water.

Attractor (color)—Unnaturally bright color in a fly pattern.

Backing (braided)—A line most commonly composed of several filaments of either nylon or Dacron braided into a single component. Used to extend fly line's length.

Bank—The higher and steeper sides above a lake or stream, usually created by water cutting or eroding the shoreline.

Bar—A mounded structure in streams and some lakes caused by accumulation of rock, sand, sediment, and dead vegetation, usually protruding out of the water or very near the surface.

Barb (hook)—The raised cut section of a hook immediately behind the point. It is designed to prevent the hook from coming out of the fish's mouth.

Barbless hook—A fly hook without a barb.

Bass—A general descriptive term for a group of larger freshwater sunfish, particularly large-mouth bass, smallmouth bass, and Kentucky or spotted bass.

Bass bug—A floating fly used for bass fly fishing.

Beaching—A method of landing a fish by coaxing or forcing it to swim or drift itself aground in the shallow water of a lake or stream shoreline.

Beaver pond—A small lake, usually less than two acres, that has been formed by the damming of a small brook or stream by beavers.

Belly—The larger midsection of a fly line. Also may refer to the curve of a fly-line midsection when wind or current pushes it into a C shape.

Bite—A term often used by fly fishers to describe the strike of a fish. *Bite* also may refer to the distance from the hook point and the extent of the bend.

Bite tippet—A short tippet of heavy monofilament or wire that prevents a sharp-toothed fish from biting the fly off the leader. Also called a *shock tippet*.

Brackish water—Water that has less salt content than true ocean salt water. Occurs most commonly where freshwater streams meet or mix with saltwater bays and estuaries.

Braided loop—A loop connector that slides over either end of the fly line and is fixed there with glue or a heat-shrink sleeve. Used for loop-to-loop connections of the leader or shooting line to the fly line.

Breakoff—The accidental or purposeful breaking of the leader tippet from a hooked fish, freeing it.

Bucktail—A streamer fly constructed from the hair of a deer's tail.

Bug—Usually refers to a floating bass fly that might imitate various large insects, frogs, mice, and so on.

Butt cap—The end of a fly-rod handle used for resting and protecting the fly rod and fly reel when stored upright. At times it is rested against the fly fisher's stomach when fighting a large fish.

Canal—A man-made, water-filled ditch used to join lakes or swamps to rivers, or to straighten and quicken the flow of a stream's runoff.

Cast—The act of delivering the fly to the fishing area with fly rod, line, and leader. *Cast* is also used as a descriptive term by English fly fishers to denote the fly leader.

Catch and release—An expression for catching fish, with immediate release alive and unharmed.

Catch-and-release net—A shallow, soft, fine-mesh, knotless dip net that enhances the ability to capture, unhook, and release a fish without harming it.

Channel—The main depression caused by flowing water (current).

Char—A group of popular freshwater fish that includes brook trout, lake trout, arctic char, and Dolly Varden.

Chenille—A popular fly-tying material consisting of fine fibers of rayon, wool, nylon, and so on that are bound together in a uniform cord with two or more twisted threads. Especially popular on underwater flies such as the Woolly Worm.

Chum line—A series of fish food pieces put into the water to attract and congregate hungry fish in a specific area near the angler.

Class tippet—A tippet that is accurately calibrated in pound test for world-record fly-fishing catches.

Clippers—A small tool used to cut and trim the fly line, leader, or tippet material.

Coaster—A local term, especially along the northeastern Atlantic coast, for a brown or brook trout that goes into brackish or salt water for a period of its life and then returns to freshwater streams to spawn.

Cold-water fish—Fish that thrive best in water temperatures ranging from 40 to 60 degrees F. For example: trout, char, grayling, and salmon.

Cool-water fish—Fish that thrive best in water temperatures ranging from 50 to 75 degrees F. For example: smallmouth bass, shad, walleye, northern pike, whitefish, striped bass.

Corkers—Rubber sandals with sharp, hard-metal cleats in their soles that are worn over waders, boots, or shoes to increase grip or traction on very slippery rock stream bottoms.

Cork rings—Rings of cork that are glued together and shaped to form the fly-rod handle.

Cove—A small water indentation in the shoreline of a lake or ocean.

Crayfish—A freshwater, lobsterlike, small crustacean very popular as fish food.

Creel—A container cooled by water evaporation, used to keep and carry dead fish.

Crossbar (fly reel)—A part of a fly-reel frame that is chiefly for structural support between the two sides. Sometimes referred to as a *post*.

Cruising (fish)—An expression describing a fish that is moving about in a lake or stream in order to find food.

Crustaceans—An important group of fresh- and saltwater aquatic invertebrates that are fed upon by many fish. Shrimp, scud, sow bugs, crabs, and crayfish are examples.

Current—The flowing or gravitational pull of water in rivers, streams, lakes, and oceans.

Dead drift—The drift of a fly downstream without action other than what is given it by the natural current flow. It means no drag.

Deer hair—Body hair, usually coarse and semi-hollow, from various deer. Used for tying many fly designs.

Density—Refers to the weight of fly line, leader, or fly compared to the weight of the water. *High density* means much heavier than water and fast sinking. *Low density* means slow sinking or even floating.

Dip net—The device used to scoop up and hold a hooked fish. Also called a *landing net*.

Double hook—A fly-hook design that has two points, barbs, and bends, and one common shank. Most commonly used for making Atlantic salmon flies.

Drag (guides)—The rod's guides and fly line create points of friction that are often referred to as *drag*.

Drag (line)—An expressive term used to describe a current or wind pull on the fly line that results in pulling the fly unnaturally over or through the water.

Drag (reel)—A part of the fly reel that adjusts the spool's tension when line is pulled off the reel by the fly fisher or a fish.

Dress—The application of waterproofing or flotant material to the fly line, leader, or fly.

Drift—Describes the path a fly travels while it is fished down the stream's current.

Dry fly—A basic fly design that floats on the water's surface. It is usually made of low-density, water-resistant materials to hold it in the water's surface film.

Dry-fly paste—A paste compound used to waterproof materials to hold them in the water's surface film.

Dry-fly spray—Aerosol spray compound used to waterproof the water-absorbent materials of a dry fly.

Dubbing—A fly-tying material consisting of natural hairs and/or synthetic fibers blended into a loose felt and used to form the body of many floating and sinking flies.

Dun—The term used to identify the first adult stage (subimago) of mayfly aquatic insects. Also a descriptive term generally referring to a gray or dull color common on mayfly duns.

Eddy—A calm, slowly swirling (upstream) water flow in a stream behind an obstruction such as a boulder, log, bar, or moss bed.

Emerger—A term to identify the stage of a natural or a fly imitation of an aquatic insect as it swims to the surface to hatch or transform from nymph or pupa to adult.

Feeding—A fish's eating or striking period.

Fighting—The act of tiring a hooked fish in preparation for landing it.

Fingerling—A general term used to describe various fish species (trout, bass, catfish, and so on.) when they are about finger-length in size.

Fishery—A body of water that sustains a healthy fish population and has potential for fly-fishing success.

Fish for fun—Catching and immediately releasing fish alive and unharmed. Usually it is illegal to keep or kill fish caught in these designated areas.

Fish locator—A common name for various electronic sonars that are used to locate fish, the structures wherein they live, their depth in the water, and the depth of the water itself. Also called a fish-finder.

Fishing vest—A vest with assorted pockets for carrying the various flies, reels, and accessories used while walking, wading, or fly fishing.

Flat—A wide shallow-water section of a lake, stream, or ocean. Flats usually have a relatively uniform smooth surface.

Flotant—Material used to waterproof fly lines, leaders, and flies.

Fly—The artificial lure used in fly fishing.

Fly design—Describes type of fly or purpose of fly.

Fly pattern—The color and material makeup of a particular fly design.

Fly tyer—A person who makes or "ties" flies for fly fishing.

Foam line—An accumulation of air bubbles on the water's surface caused by water turbulence, winds, tides, or currents. Fish often concentrate and feed under foam lines.

Freestone stream—A stream that has a relatively high bottom gradient and so is swift flowing made up mostly of coarse gravel or rubble and whose source of water is mainly runoff rain and melting snow.

Fresh water—Water with little or no salt content. It also refers to fish species that are adapted only to freshwater environs.

Fry—The first stage of development of a fish after hatching from the egg or live birth. Usually from $1/2$ to 2 inches in length.

Gaff—A hook-and-handle tool used to hook and capture larger fish. Also refers to the act of hooking and capturing a fish once it has been tired with rod and reel.

Game fish—A general term used to denote those species of fish that will readily strike or attack an artificial lure or fly. Also deals with the ability and willingness of the fish to fight very hard after it is hooked.

Gap—The distance between the hook shank and the point.

Gill—The respiratory organ of a water-breathing fish, located just behind the head.

Giving tip—Holding the rod tip forward and high to provide maximum shock absorption to prevent the leader's tippet from breaking and the fly from being pulled out of the fish's mouth.

Grab—A term often used to describe a brief period fish go through when they are willing to strike a fly.

Grain—The unit of measurement used for calibrating fly-line weights.

Grease—The application of paste or fly dressing to line to enhance flotation.

Hackle—Usually neck and back feathers of a chicken; however, it can also be from other chickenlike birds such as grouse or partridge.

Handle (reel)—A crank on a fly-reel spool used for reeling the fly line onto the fly reel.

Handle (rod)—The grip used for holding the fly rod while casting, fishing, and fighting a fish.

Hauling—A method of increasing fly-line speed during pickup, backward, or forward casting. It is accomplished by the hand pulling on the fly line between the rod's stripper guide and the fly reel.

Hold—A place where a fish, such as a salmon, trout, or bass, rests or remains stationary for a period of time.

Holding fish—Describes a fish that remains in a particular spot in a lake or stream.

Hook barb—The raised metal slice off the hook point and bend. The barb helps prevent the hook from backing out of the fish's mouth tissue.

Hook bend—The curved or bent section just behind the hook shank.

Hook eye—The closed loop part of a fly hook to which the leader tip or tippet is attached.

Hook (fly)—The device used to hold a fish that strikes or attempts to eat the fly.

Hook(-ing) fish—Setting the hook in a fish's mouth tissue after the fish has struck.

Hookkeeper—The small clip or eyelet at the front of the fly-rod handle used to store the fly when not in use.

Hook point—The needlelike point on the end of the hook bend. It enhances faster penetration into the fish's mouth tissue.

Hook shank—The length of the fly hook exclusive of its eye and bend and point. Generally it is the section to which the fly materials are tied.

Hook size—The distance or amount of gap on a fly hook or fly. Also refers to the overall length and size of wire the hook is made from. Generally hook sizes range from largest #5/0 to smallest #36.

Immature insect—Refers to insects that have not reached sexual maturity or full growth.

Inlet—The area of a lake, pond, or ocean where a stream flows in.

Jack—A common term usually referring to one- or two-year-old sexually mature male salmon or trout that join older fish in their spawning run.

Jump—When a hooked fish comes up out of the water in an attempt to shake the hook or break the leader.

Kick boat—A small, one-person fishing craft that is propelled by the angler's legs and swimfins. Some kick boats have oars as a second method of propulsion.

Knotless—A leader that has no knots tied in it to join different-sized sections or tippets.

Land(-ing)—Capturing a hooked fish after it has become tired.

Larva—A term denoting the worm or grublike stage between the egg and pupa of the caddis and midge aquatic insects. Also the common descriptive term of the artificial-fly imitation of the larva.

Leader—The transparent part of the fly-fishing line between the fly line and fly. It may include the tippet section.

Leader straightener—A rubber or leather pad used to heat and straighten the coils from a leader.

Leader wallet—A convenient pocketed container for storage of extra leaders to be carried while fly fishing.

Leech—A bloodsucking, wormlike aquatic invertebrate or a fly imitating it.

Levels—The amount of water or depth of a stream or lake.

Line—Short expression for *fly line*. When the fly line scares a fish it is commonly referred to as *lining* it.

Line guard—The part of a fly reel that the fly line passes through or over as it is wound on or off the reel spool. It acts as a guide and reduces wear from line friction.

Loop—The general term describing the U shape of the fly line as it unrolls forward or backward during the casting cycle.

Loop to loop—An expression used to describe the joining of the fly line to the leader or leader to tippet, where a closed loop in each is joined to make the other connection.

Lure—An imitation fish food with one or more hooks on it. As a verb it refers to attracting a fish to strike a fly.

Manipulate—Generally refers to more intricate fly presentation and actions accomplished with fly rods of 9 feet or longer.

Mature insect—Insects that have reached sexual maturity or full growth.

Matuka—Generally refers to a special fly design in which feathers are uniquely wrapped to the length of a hook shank and/or body of a fly so that they appear as part of the body. The word *Matuka* originated from a bird, the matukar, whose feathers were popularly used for this type of fly.

Meadow stream—A low-gradient stream that flows in a meandering course mainly through meadows or valleys.

Mending—The act of lifting or rolling the fly line with the rod to reposition it in order to avoid fly drag due to current speeds or wind.

Mesh—The net bag or seine of a dip net or landing net.

Minnow—A general term used for many species of smaller fishes (1 to 6 inches long), as well as the same sizes of immature larger fish.

Monofilament—A single filament or strand of nylon used for fishing line, leader, or tippet material.

Moss bed—A large underwater growth of aquatic plants.

Mudding—The term used to describe a fish stirring up a visible cloud of mud or silt as it feeds and swims on the bottom.

Muddler—A very popular and effective type of artificial fly that has a large, clipped deer hair head and usually incorporates hair and feathers for its body parts.

Neck—A long, narrow body of water usually found at a stream's inlet to a lake.

Net—Refers to the act of landing a fish with a dip net or landing net.

Neutral color—Color and pattern of a fly or natural food that does not contrast with its surroundings.

No-kill—A fishery policy of catching and releasing unharmed live fish.

Non-gamefish—A general term used to describe those species of fish that never or seldom strike or attack artificial lures or flies.

Nymph—Refers to the water-breathing or immature stage of aquatic insects. Also a fly that imitates these insects.

Nymphing—Fly fishing with aquatic nymph imitations. Also used to describe a fish that is foraging for aquatic nymphs.

Outlet—That part of a lake where water flows out.

Palming the reel—The application of a palm against the fly reel's outer spool flange to add extra drag pressure on a fish pulling line off the fly reel.

Panfish—A large group of abundant freshwater gamefish species, generally under 2 pounds in weight. Included are sunfish, bluegill, yellow perch, white bass, crappie, to name a few.

Parr—The second stage of development of salmonoids, usually termed fingerlings. Term comes from large dark bands of oval marks on their sides.

Perch—A group of fish including the yellow perch, white perch, darter, and walleye pike.

Pickup—The lifting of a fly line, leader, and fly off the water as the backcast is begun.

Pike—A group of cold and cool freshwater gamefish including northern pike, pickerel, and muskie. Sometimes walleye pike (which is not a true pike but a perch) is included.

Pocket—A depression in the bottom of a stream located in the riffle or run of a stream.

Pocket water—A series of bottom depressions or pockets in a stream riffle or run section.

Point—Refers to the narrow, pointed section of land that juts out into a lake or stream.

Polaroids—A popular term for sunglasses that polarize or filter out certain angles of light rays. They reduce reflective sunlight off water so fish beneath are more easily seen.

Pond—Usually refers to a small lake less than five acres in surface area, except in Maine, where it is often used interchangeably with *lake*.

Pound test—Refers to the strength of a fishing line, leader, or tippet. Sometimes called *breaking strength* or *test*.

Power (rod)—The degree of efficiency a rod has in casting, hooking, and landing a fish.

Predator fish—A fish that eats live fish, insects, and other animals.

Presentation—The placement of the fly on or below the water. Also describes the fly's path and action on the water.

Pressure (rod)—How hard a fly fisher pulls, restricts, or fights a hooked fish with the fly rod, reel, and leader determines the amount of pressure being used.

Pumping a fish—Pulling a large fish by using a pumping or rod-butt-lifting action as the fish sounds or pulls away. As the rod is quickly lowered after the pump-up, the reel takes up the line gained on the fish.

Pupa—Generally refers to the stage between larva and adult of the caddis and midge aquatic insects. Also common descriptive term used for the artificial fly imitation of the same insects.

Putting down—Fish that have been scared by the fly fisher and stop feeding have been *put down*.

Put and take—A fishery management policy that involves artificial stocking of catchable fish and encouragement of killing and removing these fish when caught.

Rapids—A section of a stream that has a high gradient and fast, rough-surfaced flowing water.

Reading water—Visually examining the surface of the water to evaluate fishing potential, depth, and fish location.

Reel—To wind in or retrieve the fly line, leader, backing, and so on. Also a short expression for *fly reel*.

Reel hand—The hand and arm used to hold or reel in the fly line. Same as *line hand*.

Reel saddle—The part of a reel that provides means for attaching the reel to the rod seat and/or handle.

Reel seat—The part of a fly rod, just behind the rod handle, where the fly reel is fastened.

Reel spool—The part of a fly reel where the line is wound and stored.

Riffle—The section of a stream where the water flows shallowly and rapidly over an irregular bottom so that the surface riffles. Also refers to a water surface slightly disturbed by the wind.

Rising fish—A fish that is visibly feeding just below or at the water's surface.

Rod blank—A fly rod before it is fitted with guides and handle or other finished fly-rod accessories.

Rod guides—Also *fly-rod guides*, the closed loop structures fastened to the fly-rod shaft that hold the fly line on the rod's length.

Roll—The movement of a fish when it arches up and down from the surface as it feeds.

Run—The fleeing swim of a fish that has been hooked and frightened. Also describes a stretch of stream just below a riffle and above a pool.

Salmon fly—An artificial fly used most commonly for Atlantic salmon. Also refers to a common name given to several larger species of stonefly aquatic insects.

Salt water—A general term used to describe the fish or fishing in salty oceans, seas, and other similar saltwater areas.

Saltwater fly—An artificial fly that is made principally to be fished in salt water. Its hook must resist salt corrosion.

Selective—Refers to the feeding habits of fish preferring special flies or special presentation of flies.

School—A group of the same species of fish swimming together.

Scud—A small shrimplike crustacean or a fly imitating it.

Shoal—A shallow-bottomed area in a lake, stream, or estuary.

Shock tippet—see *Bite tippet.*

Shocking the tip—This happens when the forward-and-down fly-casting stroke is begun too quickly and with too much acceleration, causing the fly-rod tip to dip back and down sharply, creating a tailing-loop cast.

Shoot(-ing)—A term referring to the fly line or shooting line that is pulled out from the force or momentum of the casting power and extended fly-line weight.

Shoreline—The area immediately adjacent to the water's edge, along lakes and streams.

Shrimp—A widely distributed, important crustacean and also its fly imitation.

Sidefinder—A special electronic sonar fish locator that detects fish on a horizontal plane (to the side) of a boat or float tube that it is mounted on.

Skater—A design of floating fly that has a very long hackle or hair around the hook to enable it to sit high or skate across the water's surface.

Slack line—When the fly line has little or no tension on it between the fly reel, the rod, and the fly.

Slough—A sluggish or nonflowing narrow, dead-ended body of water usually created by a stream changing to a new path or channel. The old channel becomes a slough if water still connects it to the stream.

Smolt—The third stage of development of sea-run salmonids (trout, salmon, char), usually in lengths of 4 to 10 inches.

Snag guard—A device on a fly that prevents the fly hook from snagging or hanging on various obstacles (rocks, logs, moss, and so on.) near or in the fishing water.

Snake guide—A simple two-footed, open, wire-loop fly-rod guide, designed principally to reduce friction and overall weight, and to hold the fly line close to the fly-rod shaft. It slightly resembles a semicoiled snake in shape.

Snelled fly—An artificial fly with a short permanent section of gut or monofilament attached to it. On the opposite end is a fixed closed loop to attach the snell to the leader.

Spawn—The act of fish reproduction. Also refers to a mass of fish eggs.

Spawning runs—The movement of a fish or a number of fish from their resident water to a more suitable area to mate and to lay their eggs.

Spillway—The outlet section of a lake where the water flows over a particular section of the dam.

Spinner—The term used to identify the second adult stage (imago) of mayfly aquatic insects. Also a small shiny metal blade that revolves on a metal wire shaft when pulled through the water to attract a fish to the fly.

Spinning—A method of lure-casting that utilizes a fixed-spool reel in which the line spins off as the weighted lure pulls it out.

Splice—The joining of two fly-line sections together.

Spook—Scaring a fish so much that it stops feeding and/or swims away and hides.

Spring creek—A stream in which the water originates from the flow of subsurface spring water.

Steelhead—A migrating rainbow trout that lives part of its life in freshwater streams and other parts in saltwater oceans or large freshwater lakes.

Steelhead fly—An artificial sinking fly designed specifically for catching steelhead.

Straightening (fly line or leader)—The removal of coils or twists in the fly line or leader caused by their storage on the fly reel.

Streamer—A subsurface fly that imitates small fish or similarly shaped natural creatures a fish might strike or eat.

Strike—A fish hitting or biting the natural food or artificial fly. Also the action a fly fisher takes with fly rod and line to set the hook in a fish's mouth.

Stringer—A length of cord, rope, or chain for retaining, keeping alive, and carrying caught fish.

Stripper guide—The first large guide on the butt section of a fly rod above the rod handle. It is designed to reduce friction and enhance casting and retrieving.

Stripping—The act of rapidly retrieving a fly and fly line that involves making a series of fast pulls on the fly line with the line hand.

Structure—Describes objects in the water that fish would live near. Used more in lake fishing than in stream fishing.

Studs—Metal protrusions on the soles of wading shoes or boots for improving footing on very slick wet rocks, ice, or the like.

Swim—The way a sinking fly moves through the water as it is being fished. It may move like a minnow or a nymph, for example, or simply swim as an attractor.

Synthetic tying materials—Fly-tying materials that are man-made; for example, Orlon, Mylar, and FisHair.

Tackle—A general term covering all equipment used in fly fishing.

Tag end—The forward end of a leader or tippet.

Tail—The caudal fin of a fish. Also refers to capturing and/or landing a hooked fish by grasping it just in front of its tail. Also the lower or end (downstream) portion of a stream pool.

Tailer—A tool for tailing (landing) fish. It has a locking loop on the handle that locks around the fish's tail.

Tailing—A term often used to describe a fish feeding in a position along the bottom in shallow water so that its tail sometimes sticks above the surface of the water.

Tailwater—A stream coming from a large man-made dam.

Tailwater trout—Trout that live in the cold-water streams below man-made dams.

Take—The fish's action in catching food or a fly.

Taper—The shape of a fly line or leader. May also be used in describing fly-rod shape.

Terrestrial insect—Insects that are land-born air breathers. Included are grasshoppers, crickets, ants, beetles, and the like.

Tide—The periodic raising and lowering of water levels in streams, lakes, and oceans due to gravitational forces or releases of impounded waters.

Tie—Describes the making of artificial flies. Also a term used to describe forming various line, leader, and fly knots.

Tippet—The small end of a leader or additional section of nylon monofilament tied to the end of the leader.

Tip-top—The fly-rod line guide that is fitted over the rod's tip end.

Treble hook—A fish hook with three bends, barbs, and points joined on a common shank.

Trolling—Fishing a fly or lure by pulling it behind a boat. Less commonly, fishing by wading or walking with the fly dragging in the water behind.

Trout—A group of very popular freshwater gamefish that live in cold, pure water. Includes rainbow trout, golden trout, brown trout, cutthroat trout, brook trout, to name a few.

Twitch—A small movement given to the fly by using the rod tip or a short fly-line strip.

Vest (Fishing vest)—A vestlike garment containing a number of various-sized pockets used to carry flies and other fishing accessory items while fly fishing.

Wading—Walking on the bottom of a stream, lake, or ocean in water no deeper than your chest.

Waders—Waterproof combination of shoes and pants used for wading.

Wading shoes—Shoes used over stocking-foot waders for wading.

Wading staff—A walking cane used to assist in wading, particularly on slick, irregular bottoms and in swift water.

Warm-water fish—Fish that thrive best in water temperatures ranging from 65 to 85 degrees F.

Water clarity—The degree of transparency water has; how far below the surface you can see an object.

Water color—Refers to a water's color tint. It is affected by suspended particles and the bottom color reflection.

Water condition—A general expression fly fishers use to describe the combination of level, temperature, and clarity.

Weed guard—A simple wire or nylon device on a fly that prevents it from hooking vegetation in the fishing area.

Wiggle nymph—A two-section, hinge-bodied, artificial nymph fly.

Wind knot—A simple but troublesome overhand knot that is accidentally tied on the fly line or leader while casting.

Woolly Worm—A design of sinking fly that has a fuzzy or woolly body, and hackle spiraled around and over the body's length. Also the larvae of terrestrial moths or butterflies.

INDEX

183